W9-BLF-208

Higher Education and State Governments:
Renewed Partnership, Cooperation, or Competition?

by Edward R. Hines

ASHE-ERIC Higher Education Report No. 5, 1988

Prepared by

Clearinghouse on Higher Education
The George Washington University

Published by

Association for the Study of
Higher Education

Jonathan D. Fife,
Series Editor

Cite as
Hines, Edward R. *Higher Education and State Governments: Renewed Partnership, Cooperation, or Competition?* ASHE-ERIC Higher Education Report No. 5. Washington, D.C.: Association for the Study of Higher Education, 1988.

Library of Congress Catalog Card Number 88-83591
ISSN 0884-0040
ISBN 0-913317-47–0

Managing Editor: Christopher Rigaux
Manuscript Editor: Barbara Fishel/Editech
Cover design by Michael David Brown, Rockville, Maryland

The ERIC Clearinghouse on Higher Education invites individuals to submit proposals for writing monographs for the Higher Education Report series. Proposals must include:
1. A detailed manuscript proposal of not more than five pages.
2. A chapter-by-chapter outline.
3. A 75-word summary to be used by several review committees for the initial screening and rating of each proposal.
4. A vita.
5. A writing sample.

ERIC Clearinghouse on Higher Education
School of Education and Human Development
The George Washington University
One Dupont Circle, Suite 630
Washington, D.C. 20036-1183

ASHE Association for the Study of Higher Education
Texas A&M University
Department of Educational Administration
Harrington Education Center
College Station, Texas 77843

This publication was prepared partially with funding from the Office of Educational Research and Improvement, U.S. Department of Education, under contract no. ED RI-88-062014. The opinions expressed in this report do not necessarily reflect the positions or policies of OERI or the Department.

EXECUTIVE SUMMARY

The 1980s and 1990s have been characterized as a period when states will be major initiators of policies for higher education. This higher education report is intended for administrators, faculty, and student leaders in higher education; for state lawmakers and staff who work with higher education; and for others desiring information about current policy issues and relationships between state government and higher education. The underlying conceptual issue throughout the report is the issue of accountability and autonomy. This issue and, more broadly, the relationship between state government and higher education are explored using a set of current policy issues, including economic development, assessment, and deregulation. In the analysis, a continuum is presented from a condition of full accountability with maximum state control to complete autonomy with minimum state control. In higher education, the most common pattern has been a state-aided approach typified by states' encouraging institutions to develop programs and services.

How Deeply Involved in Higher Education Are Governors?
Economic development and assessment provide clear evidence of the extent to which state lawmakers, especially governors, have become deeply involved in higher education. In most states, the governor has become the single most important person in higher education (Kerr 1985). This report explores gubernatorial involvement in higher education, analyzes governors' formal powers and how those powers affect higher education, and illustrates how structurally weak governors have made significant accomplishments in education.

What Is the Extent of State-Level Lobbying for Higher Education?
Higher education lobbying has increased at both state and federal levels. This report analyzes examples of aggressive state-level lobbying, showing how campuses and higher education systems have increased their presence in state capitals, including a successful grass-roots lobbying effort in Texas to increase support of higher education. The downside of lobbying is discussed, with illustrations of conflicts of interest and alignments with political action committees.

What Is the Effect of the Reform Movement In Higher Education?

This report shows how current reform differs from previous efforts because of the involvement of strong external actors, such as governors and legislators. In a number of analyses of reform, quality and excellence, the link between education and economic development, finance, governance, and clarification of institutional missions emerge as key issues. Governors are the catalysts in reform of higher education, and they along with legislative leaders have appointed blue ribbon commissions and ad hoc groups to study the restructuring of governance and other issues.

How Effective Are Blue Ribbon Commissions?

Discontent with higher education systems has resulted in blue ribbon commissions and ad hoc study groups in a majority of the states in the 1980s. Commissions often focus on the structure of state-level governance. States, assuming that structural change will lead to changes in other areas, may be disappointed to find their problems unresolved. Structure is a means, not an end. States' experiences with such restructuring have led to several observations. A clear vision for higher education in the state and an understanding of the obstacles to achieving that vision are necessary. Organizational structure is a means to other policy goals. The entire process involving higher education policy needs to be examined. No perfect or preferred model of structure and organization exists (McGuinness 1986).

How Important Is Incentive Financing To Colleges and Universities?

New developments in state finance of higher education have created important mechanisms to get new money to campuses—including strategies promoting economic development, excellence, and increased productivity. One strategy uses incentive financing to link levels of appropriation to measurable outcomes, exemplified by the Tennessee Performance Funding Project. Another strategy includes states' using "set-aside" funds to reward exemplary institutional practices.

Why Is Economic Development Such a Critical Policy Issue?

States are providing financial support to higher education in areas like training, technological development, and collaboration with business and industry. Governors are interested in higher education because of its demonstrated link to economic development. Certain concerns have arisen, however, about the effectiveness of economic development. One issue is how to measure effectiveness, another is the use of job creation as a measure of effectiveness, and still another concerns the influence of economic development on the longer-term relationship between government and higher education. The Ben Franklin Partnership in Pennsylvania compellingly illustrates a successful relationship in economic development between government and higher education: over 19,500 persons retrained in technology application, 439 new technology-based firms established, 390 companies expanded, over 10,600 manufacturing jobs created or retained, $100 million invested by the commonwealth, and $350 million invested by the private sector (Leventhal 1988).

What Is the Relationship between Government and Higher Education in Assessment?

Assessment is a policy issue of major interest to state lawmakers. In the *Governors' 1991 Report on Education*, one task force focused on quality and studied ways to demonstrate improved learning, student outcomes, and program effectiveness (National Governors' Association 1986). The Education Commission of the States, comprised of governmental and educational leaders nationwide, sponsored a number of efforts focused on assessment in higher education. An ECS survey found that by 1987, two-thirds of the states had initiated assessment, with some states engaged in a monitoring role while campuses provide leadership in assessment. Other states took a more active role in promoting and facilitating assessment. A third group of states actively designed and implemented assessment programs. Decisions to move ahead with assessment, however, must be debated and resolved on each individual campus.

How Important Is State Leadership in Higher Education?

Traditionally, higher education has been decentralized and self-governing, and most critical decisions affecting colleges and universities have been made on campus. Today, however, state-level decisions for higher education are critical. Governors and legislators are more involved in higher education than ever before. The state higher education agency is in a key position to provide leadership on pressing policy issues to campus chief executive officers as well as to state lawmakers. State higher education executive officers must function effectively in both political and higher education policy arenas. Governing boards must speak for higher education and serve as buffers against political pressure.

To What Extent Is Authority Being Decentralized?
Examples of state decisions to deregulate higher education and restore flexibility to campus management include decisions in Colorado, Connecticut, Kentucky, Maryland, New Jersey, and New York, among other states. This report reviews research that concludes that regulation is caused by political factors while quality is the result of state investment (Volkwein 1989). The debate over accountability versus autonomy is discussed as it relates to the extent to which centralization of authority and political decisions have been increasingly intrusive in higher education in the 1980s. Intrusion is viewed as having bureaucratic, political, and ideological aspects (Newman 1987a).

How Critical Are Concerns about Minorities?
Concerns about minorities present higher education with a great challenge and encompass a number of specific policy issues—admitting minority students, increasing retention, improving graduation rates, and hiring more minority administrators, faculty, and staff. State higher education executive officers have made initial steps in this direction, working closely with state leaders as well as with campus officials. While state leaders can serve as catalysts in identifying specific problems and mobilizing action toward goals, individual campuses must become involved in implementing solutions to improve conditions and increase opportunities for minorities.

What Should Be the Role of State Government In Higher Education?
It is not possible to formulate an ideal role for government that prescribes consistent action and carries across all policy issues. In some cases, a "state agency" role for government may be appropriate. In other instances, a state agency role would be too intrusive and would be rejected by higher education leaders. The relationship between government and higher education has changed markedly in recent years. The role of government has evolved from providing financial support for a basic level of educational services to serving as a partner with higher edu-

cation in the resolution of key policy issues. State government leaders are integrally involved in higher education, and governors especially play key roles in economic development and assessment of outcomes. Lawmakers' roles range from near total involvement to virtually no involvement.

What Limits Exist on State Governments' Action in Higher Education?

Government cannot be expected to define and carry out an appropriate role in all areas, because on some occasions, government will be intrusive. It is during such times that higher education, in particular the state higher education agency, must be insightful enough to discern the problem and be courageous enough to call for corrections. Neither partner, however, can define the relationship unilaterally. State higher education executive officers and their staffs serve in a difficult buffer role— simultaneously coexisting in two related but different worlds. Points of intersection occur at annual hearings before budget examiners and legislative fiscal committees on issues of substance, including the role of higher education in economic development and the role of government in assessing learning outcomes and institutional productivity. Some may claim that higher education has no role in economic development and that the state has no role in assessment. Such views harken back to a time when government and higher education functioned in separate worlds, however. Now the worlds are interrelated, and they intersect more often than not. Higher education must define the limits of its autonomy and must call for redress when government becomes intrusive. When that situation occurs, government and higher education will be able to maintain a dynamic partnership.

ADVISORY BOARD

Roger G. Baldwin
Assistant Professor of Education
College of William and Mary

Carol M. Boyer
Senior Policy Analyst for Higher Education
Education Commission of the States

Clifton F. Conrad
Professor of Higher Education
Department of Educational Administration
University of Wisconsin–Madison

Elaine H. El-Khawas
Vice President
Policy Analysis and Research
American Council on Education

Martin Finkelstein
Associate Professor of Higher Education Administration
Seton Hall University

Carol Everly Floyd
Associate Vice Chancellor for Academic Affairs
Board of Regents of the Regency Universities System
State of Illinois

George D. Kuh
Professor of Higher Education
School of Education
Indiana University

Yvonna S. Lincoln
Associate Professor of Higher Education
University of Kansas

Richard F. Wilson
Associate Chancellor
University of Illinois

Ami Zusman
Principal Analyst, Academic Affairs
University of California

CONSULTING EDITORS

Charles Adams
Director, The Inquiry Program
Center for the Study of Adult and Higher Education
University of Massachusetts

Ann E. Austin
Research Assistant Professor
Vanderbilt University

Trudy W. Banta
Research Professor
University of Tennessee

Robert J. Barak
Deputy Executive Secretary
Director of Academic Affairs and Research
Iowa Board of Regents

Robert Berdahl
Professor of Higher Education
University of Maryland

Kenneth A. Bruffee
Director, The Scholars Program
Brooklyn College of the City University of New York

L. Leon Campbell
Provost and Vice President for Academic Affairs
University of Delaware

Ellen Earle Chaffee
Associate Commissioner for Academic Affairs
North Dakota State Board of Higher Education

Robert Paul Churchill
Chair and Associate Professor
Department of Philosophy
George Washington University

Charles S. Claxton
Associate Professor
Center for the Study of Higher Education
Memphis State University

Susan Cohen
Associate, Project for Collaborative Learning
Lesley College

Peter T. Ewell
Senior Associate
National Center for Higher Education Management Systems

Reynolds Ferrante
Professor of Higher Education
George Washington University

Zelda F. Gamson
Director
New England Resource Center for Higher Education

J. Wade Gilley
Senior Vice President
George Mason University

Judy Diane Grace
Director of Research
Council for Advancement and Support of Education

Milton Greenberg
Provost
American University

Judith Dozier Hackman
Associate Dean
Yale University

Paul W. Hartman
Vice Chancellor for University Relations and Development
Texas Christian University

James C. Hearn
Associate Professor
University of Minnesota

Evelyn Hively
Vice President for Academic Programs
American Association of State Colleges and Universities

Paul Jedamus
Professor
University of Colorado

George Keller
Senior Vice President
The Barton-Gillet Company

Oscar T. Lenning
Vice President for Academic Affairs
Robert Wesleyan College

Charles J. McClain
President
Northeast Missouri State University

Judith B. McLaughlin
Research Associate on Education and Sociology
Harvard University

Marcia Mentkowski
Director of Research and Evaluation
Professor of Psychology
Alverno College

Richard I. Miller
Professor, Higher Education
Ohio University

James R. Mingle
Executive Director
State Higher Education Executive Officers

James L. Morrison
Professor
University of North Carolina

Elizabeth M. Nuss
Executive Director
National Association of Student Personnel Administrators

Robert L. Payton
Director, Center on Philanthropy
Indiana University

Karen T. Romer
Associate Dean for Academic Affairs
Brown University

Jack E. Rossmann
Professor of Psychology
Macalester College

Donald M. Sacken
Associate Professor
University of Arizona

Robert A. Scott
President
Ramapo College of New Jersey

J. Fredericks Volkwein
Director of Institutional Research
State University of New York at Albany

William R. Whipple
Director, Honors Program
University of Maine

CONTENTS

ACKNOWLEDGMENTS

This higher education report was prepared during a sabbatical leave granted by Illinois State University. I thank Aims McGuinness and Rochelle Torscher of the Education Commission of the States, the ERIC staff, and Glenn Gritzmacher, Helga Whitcomb, and Gwen Pruyne of Illinois State University. A number of recognized scholars, including four anonymous reviewers, were helpful in identifying sources and providing suggestions. Special appreciation is extended to the late Roald F. Campbell and to Professor Tim L. Mazzoni, Jr., then at Ohio State University, who were instrumental in my study of state government and higher education.

FOREWORD

Four undeniable conditions affect public higher education today. First, the majority of college students attend state supported institutions. Second, there is a general dissatisfaction with the quality of output from higher education institutions. Third, in the foreseeable future there will be more competition for public funds, especially from areas such as social security, Medicare and Medicaid, day care, and crime prevention. Fourth, the public holds elected officials accountable for how well public monies are spent.

These factors translate into the undeniable fact that public colleges must continue to be concerned with their relationships with state government if they are to meet public expectations and to receive sufficient public funding. This will call for not only strong leadership, but also statesmanship. The days of competition between, and separation from, state governments and public institutions have passed. Administrative leaders must, of necessity, be concerned with institution-state relations; it is now even more critical that middle management and faculty leaders also be concerned. How expectations are set, how successfully faculties perform, how well curriculum innovations address public sensitivities—these areas and others are affected by the degree to which cooperation and partnerships have been developed.

One of the major failings of public institutions is the reluctance of upper-level administrators to involve middle management and faculty in interactions with the state. If all levels communicate better with public agencies, then chances are improved for sufficient funds to support the institution's mission, and better understanding of its limitations. All this creates more realistic expectations.

This report, written by Edward Hines of the Center for Higher Education at Illinois State University, views the state-institutional relationship as one that straddles accountability and autonomy. The author uses several current issues to illustrate strengths and weaknesses of different systems. He also examines carefully the role of state leadership.

The relationship between state governments and institutions of higher education is continually evolving. The choice for administrators and faculty is twofold: to be players in the redefining of the relationship, or merely to be spectators awaiting the outcome.

Jonathan D. Fife
Professor and Director
ERIC Clearinghouse on Higher Education
School of Education and Human Development
The George Washington University

INTRODUCTION

The particular perspective of this report on major policy issues in which state governments and higher education have common interests—accountability and autonomy, statewide coordination, governance, finance (all commonly found in the literature), gubernatorial involvement in higher education, lobbying, reform, minorities, blue ribbon commissions, deregulation, incentive financing, economic development, and assessment (more recent developments)—includes the extent of involvement of state government in higher education and the relationship between state governments and higher education in each issue. The purpose of this monograph is to identify policy issues in which states and higher education are involved, to analyze the relationship between government and higher education on the issues, to reassess the extent to which campus autonomy may have diminished in recent years, and to begin to explore future directions in the evolving relationship between state governments and higher education.

Most of the literature included in this monograph is from the 1980s, because a series of policy issues have arisen in this decade that are influencing the relationship between state governments and higher education, among them economic development, assessment, and deregulation. To the extent possible, less widely published sources—unpublished reports, analyses, and commentaries; material published in limited quantities and not available in all academic and government libraries; and doctoral dissertations—are included in this report (although doctoral dissertations receive limited coverage and should be used by those wishing to do additional research).

Two sources of information warrant special mention. The report uses a number of state reports and studies, especially the section on state leadership in higher education. The state files located at the Education Commission of the States and the Office of the State Higher Education Executive Officers in Denver were especially valuable. The other source used extensively in this monograph is *The Chronicle of Higher Education*, in particular the section on government and politics. Coverage of state-level political and policy issues increased considerably in the mid-1980s, offering scholars and researchers valuable information and insightful perspectives about state governments and higher education.

STATE LEADERSHIP IN HIGHER EDUCATION

The focus of this section is on state-level leadership in higher education, including key actors and agencies inside and outside higher education. Issues include state higher education agencies, governing boards, governors and legislators, lobbying at the state level, and deregulation. The section also covers the reports of blue ribbon commissions in three states, illustrating a range of approaches such ad hoc study groups use in examining higher education.

The State-Level Higher Education Agency

The number of statewide coordinating and governance structures in higher education has grown rapidly; some form of either structure exists in all states except Wyoming. Despite the fact that one can find numerous descriptions of coordination and governance, the basis of their authority, and the varying types of coordinating boards, state leaders have again returned to this topic in the 1980s, revisiting themes dealing with campus autonomy, public accountability, the centralization of state-level authority, and the proper balance between state and campus authority.

Concerns about statewide coordination and governance appear to emanate from discontent with existing systems and with emerging policy issues in the states (Mingle 1988). In many states, conflicts have developed around educationally underserved areas experiencing rapid population growth and needing access to graduate and professional programs. Senior colleges exhibit too few differences in mission and purpose. "To many governors and legislators, all institutions look and sound alike and compete for the same programs and students" (Mingle 1988, p. 3). Lawmakers wonder whether all programs offered are needed in all institutions. At the same time, needs may be unmet that the state or the campus could fulfill. When campuses choose not to become involved, policy makers sometimes turn to state boards. If state boards do not become involved, lawmakers' continued support for higher education may be jeopardized; if they become too involved, however, campuses become critical of their intrusiveness. One current example is the proliferation of incentive funding proposals while the overall budget base is reduced. Lawmakers can view state boards as resisting efforts to fund, measure, and encourage quality in higher education. Finally, state boards have long been subject to criticism about being overly bureaucratic, primarily because of their standardizing procedures for submitting proposals, for-

If state boards do not become involved, lawmakers' continued support for higher education may be jeopardized; if they become too involved, however, campuses become critical of their intrusiveness.

mulating budgets, and reporting information. The campus view of state higher education agencies may be even more negative, however. The staffs of state boards have been identified as apprehensive of mistakes, consummate rational planners, unreceptive to innovation, antithetical to the process of change, distrustful of those capable of innovation, and conservative in use of data (Gilley, Fulmer, and Reithlingshoefer 1986).

Governing and coordinating boards differ in their authority (Millett 1984), and both have advantages and disadvantages. Governing boards have authority not found in coordinating boards in three areas: authority over how individual campuses are governed, including the appointment and evaluation of the campus president; authority to intervene in the internal affairs of campuses under their jurisdiction; and authority over how campus budgets are carried out and managed. Advantages of the governing structure include its involvement in campus concerns, such as defining campus missions, approving admission standards, determining tuition and fees, and establishing the organizational structure for the campus. Governing boards select the chief administrative officer of the campus, establish the operating budget, and plan for capital improvements. Disadvantages, on the other hand, include the fact that board members may perceive themselves as more closely aligned with campuses than with state government—which may not ingratiate governing boards with governors and legislators. Some governing boards have difficult relationships with certain legislators, in which the legislator intervenes inappropriately in campus affairs or individual board members act inappropriately. The potential always exists that statewide governing boards are too far removed from the concerns and activities of individual campuses, which can present problems for relations between campuses and the governing board. Governing boards may have difficulty serving as the state-level planning agency for higher education. The focus of the governing board may exclude key segments of higher education, such as private institutions or community colleges.

Coordinating boards also have distinct advantages and disadvantages (Millett 1984). A major advantage is the broadly based scope of authority of coordinating boards and their ability to relate to many segments of higher education, including the private sector. Another advantage is that coordinating boards have specific powers in particular areas, usually including the preparation of a state master plan for higher education, approval and disapproval of new degree programs, and recommending state appropriations for operating and capital budgets. A third advantage is that coordinating boards, more so than governing boards, are able to identify with state government. Fourth, coordinating boards have no management authority over individual campuses and thus tend not to become as embroiled in campus matters as do governing boards.

Disadvantages of coordinating boards often emanate from external actors like governors and legislators who influence or make decisions affecting master plans, academic programs, and requests for appropriations. The coordinating board's lack of influence over campuses can lead to campus presidents' acting on their own at inappropriate times. Another disadvantage is that under a coordinating board, institutional governing boards and presidents may act independently, showing little concern for the coordinating board. Further, coordinating boards tend not to have their own political constituency. And coordinating boards may have an uncertain relationship with governors and legislators, primarily because in most instances appointment to the coordinating board involves overlapping terms; thus, a governor would be unable to appoint an entire board within a single term of office. Therefore, coordinating boards may be too insulated from primary political actors.

The question of coordination versus governance leads to a debate that was prevalent in the 1960s and 1970s. Since 1970, Massachusetts, North Carolina, and Wisconsin have adopted statewide consolidated governing boards. In 1988, Maryland higher education was reorganized, with a commission replacing the existing state board for higher education, a cabinet-level secretary of education appointed by the governor to replace the commissioner of higher education, and an enhanced governing board for the University of Maryland, including 11 of the 13 public four-year campuses. More than 15 other states decided to strengthen the existing coordinating board and to maintain a separate system of governance that is perceived to be closer to the campus (McGuinness 1986).

Thus, there is no one best way to organize a state structure for higher education (Callan 1982). The most significant determinants, however, are those not included in most debates about coordinating versus governing boards—the personal disposition of the governor and legislative leaders toward higher education, the experience of those leaders with higher education, the leadership of the state higher education agency and campus presi-

dents, compatibility between campus leaders and state leaders, and the place of higher education in the state's political culture. Critical issues include whether the public sector has excess capacity, the contribution of higher education toward the state's priorities in areas like economic development and manpower training, and whether the segments of higher education—public, private, two-year colleges, four-year colleges, research universities, and nonresearch universities—show rancor or cooperation. "The conditions in each state determine form and powers" (Glenny 1985, p. 13). In some states, the provision of educational services to adults and the integration of vocational-technical education with other sectors of education can be critical policy issues (Cross and McCartan 1984). If the education enterprise is badly fragmented and if the general environment is dominated by win-lose conditions, then higher education may have a difficult time in the political arena.

> *No state-supported institution anywhere exists apart from the state [that] created it and whose public interest it exists to serve. By the same token, no state coordinating agency, or any other agency of government for that matter, serves the great goals of efficiency, economy, and accountability unless it has a sophisticated and sensitive grasp of the transcendent importance of quality education, in all its rich and varied meanings. . . . Plainly the task ahead is to develop consultative relationships that bring the legitimate concerns of state agencies into shared perspectives. Warfare is too costly. Moreover, in most states both the universities and the state higher education agency share—at the deepest level of conviction—those multiple goals symbolized by words such as equity, efficiency, economy, excellence, pluralism, diversity, and the like* (Berdahl 1980, p. 13).

State higher education executive officers

The State Higher Education Executive Officers' Association, in existence since 1954, is comprised of men and women who occupy positions of leadership in state higher education systems. The state higher education executive officer (SHEEO) has been described as a person of critical importance: "No other position, at least in *public* higher education, is as critical to the resolution of such conflicts or the shaping of state higher education profiles" (Pettit and Kirkpatrick 1984b, p. 5). The SHEEO presides over a staff of individuals in a coordinating o a governing board who work in budgeting, academic programs, management information systems, planning, institutional research, and governmental liaison.

The state higher education agency is the intermediary between state government and the campus. Sometimes it is possible to get embroiled with details of coordination versus governance. SHEEOs have opportunities to exercise leadership on behalf of higher education, but the strains on SHEEOs and their agencies can be a dominant factor in their potential effectiveness (Pettit and Kirkpatrick 1984a). In many respects, SHEEOs and their staffs work in a no-man's-land, because these agencies are located at the nexus of competing interests and values. On the one hand, they are spokesmen for individual campuses, presidents, faculty, and student leaders. On the other, those external to higher education, especially governors and legislators, look to SHEEOs and state-level agencies as the advocates of higher education who will exercise the appropriate degree of control over campus officials who articulate positions on behalf of their own campus.

The continuum shown in figure 1 can be used to identify the position of SHEEOs relative to external and campus authority. According to the figure, governors' and legislators' primary responsibilities are to implement state policy, and campus chief executive officers (CEOs) are responsible for protecting institutional autonomy and advancing the interests of the campus. System "heads" and CEOs include those individuals heading a multicampus institution or system governing board. They are viewed as having less campus identification than a campus CEO and more identification with the broader public. SHEEOs are those state higher education agency heads who function at the apex of coordinating boards ("coordinating board executives" in the figure) or head governing boards ("state system CEOs"). The "system's character" is the distinguishing feature of the system, which feature is the relationship between the CEO of the system and the CEO of the campus (Pettit 1987). Key points on the continuum range from maximum accountability, where governors and legislators exercise great influence over higher education, to maximum autonomy, with the campus exercising great influence. Adjacent to maximum accountability, or a public interest model, are statewide coordinating boards that function as state agencies on behalf of higher education. Next come consolidated governing boards with CEOs not having line authority over campus presidents. Next are consolidated governing boards with stronger chief executives like commissioners, chancellors, and presidents with line authority over campuses. Closer to the campus end of the continuum are multicampus systems with less than statewide jurisdiction. The final slot contains autonomous individual campuses with a president as the CEO.

A number of factors impede "the system executive's shaping and sustaining a visible and legitimate presence conducive to meeting administrative responsibilities" (Pettit 1987, p. 198). One factor is lack of identity because, unlike institutions, systems do not have a physical entity and a broader name recognition. A higher education system is more of an abstraction. Another impediment is one of constituency; a campus has defined constituencies, while system heads have contacts with a limited array of campus officials, often excluding most students, faculty, and lower administrative staff. Third, system heads have more limited ceremonial functions and responsibilities than do campus presidents so that when they are involved,

FIGURE 1
CHIEF DECISION MAKERS IN
PUBLIC HIGHER EDUCATION SYSTEMS

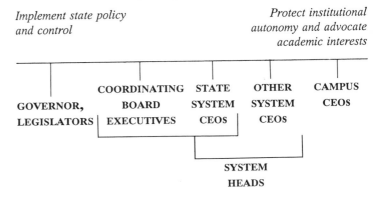

Whose primary responsibility is to:

Implement state policy and control

Protect institutional autonomy and advocate academic interests

GOVERNOR, LEGISLATORS

COORDINATING BOARD EXECUTIVES

STATE SYSTEM CEOS

OTHER SYSTEM CEOS

CAMPUS CEOS

SYSTEM HEADS

SHEEOS[a]

[a]A SHEEO can be head of a coordinating board, governing board, or a higher education agency or system.

Source: Pettit 1987, p. 197.

it is merely to serve as figureheads. Finally, legitimacy is a generalized problem. System heads may not be viewed as legitimate authority figures on campuses—necessary ceremonial figureheads perhaps, but not legitimate CEOs—creating role strain and ambiguity for them.

An analysis of the appointment of new system heads in three states points out several trends (Jaschik 1987n). First, the system head must be familiar with higher education in the state, and his or her name must be recognizable in both the higher education and the state government communities. Second, the system head must focus on critical issues in higher education, create a vision for higher education, and help move the system forward. The system head cannot be perceived as a person oriented toward preserving the status quo; a sense of forward momentum is critical. Third, the system head needs to have a sense of political acumen, to be familiar and comfortable working in the political arena, to be adept at using the political process to the benefit of higher education, and not to lose sight of the links needed with campuses. The system head needs to be a member of the higher education community or to be accepted therein yet able to function in the political arena. Finally, the system head needs to be a risk taker to be able to formulate a vision for higher education yet must know when to avoid or to reduce counterproductive controversies.

Governance is not an end in itself; rather, it is a means or one precondition to a system of postsecondary education in a state (Callan 1982). Postsecondary education can function as a system only after critical issues and state-specific problems have been identified, after goals for the higher education system have been articulated, and after state and education leaders alike have decided upon a structure suitable to the state.

Blue ribbon commissions
Special commissions and special study groups have been primary means of evaluating and examining the state-level structure and organization of higher education, especially when they involve shorter-range decision making and constituent groups inside and outside higher education (Folger and Berdahl 1988). These blue ribbon commissions, as they are commonly called, are comprised of eminent individuals and are given a purpose, time frame, and operational guidelines. Between 1965 and 1983, 48 such special commissions were established by governors or legislatures in 25 states (Johnson and Marcus 1986).

From 1980 to 1986, however—in one-third the amount of time—40 special commissions focused on higher education in the states (McGuinness 1986).

It is clear that some blue ribbon commissions are more successful than others, and certain elements contribute to their success: a manageable task, sufficient time to complete the study, a knowledgeable staff that is adequately sized, appropriate outside experts, favorable relations with the media, and commissioners who are involved in implementing recommendations (Johnson and Marcus 1986). Commissions are not likely to be effective when they must study complex problems not easily solved, they have little or no formal power, the time frame for study is too short, and they are broadly representative of diverse interests (Peterson 1983). An analysis of the reform movement in higher education suggested that little evidence demonstrates that reports by ad hoc committees enhance quality and that use of such committees raises questions about the ability of higher education to examine itself. Ad hoc committees may be able to provide starting points for identifying policy problems, but real reform will require higher education to address more fundamental issues (Mitchell 1987). Based on their examination of higher education commissions in seven states in the 1980s, Folger and Berdahl (1988) questioned a number of factors thought to be associated with successful commissions. Having sufficient time to complete the study and hiring external consultants does not guarantee success. Timing and the manner of release of the commission's work to the public can be critical factors. A match must be made between the purpose of a special commission and the qualifications of both commissioners and staff. Study commissions may tend to have little effect on fiscal issues, because so many groups must become involved in fiscal decision making. Blue ribbon groups may be more helpful at defining policy issues than actually solving problems or formulating specific solutions.

Those considering using a special study commission should heed several suggestions (McGuinness 1986). A commission should consider all sectors of postsecondary education and implications for elementary and secondary education. Commissions should examine more than a few elements and consider ways in which recommendations in one area can affect other areas. For instance, state aid formulas for community colleges can affect other elements, such as the cost of tuition in four-year colleges, student aid, loans, and even state appropriations.

At the same time, a commission cannot study all conceivable issues related to a problem; a manageable number of strategic issues should be selected. Some issues can be addressed immediately; others may require study over a longer time. Some issues are essential to campus concerns; others affect entire higher education systems.

Analysis of three states

While detailed analysis of the reports of blue ribbon commissions is beyond the scope of this report and the particular recommendations contained in a report reflect the conditions of a particular state at a particular time, this section offers a brief analysis of blue ribbon commissions examining higher education in Maryland, Michigan, and Rhode Island. These cases exemplify a larger number of states considering a particular structural configuration for higher education. Maryland, for instance, is one of a number of states where an enhanced coordinating board, a "superboard," was under consideration until a major reorganization in 1988. Rhode Island illustrates a number of states where statewide boards function essentially as governing bodies for separate institutions, with little attention to questions regarding how institutions should relate to each other in meeting the state's needs. These boards have operated with minimal support staff, instead depending on working relationships among campus CEOs. Such arrangements more recently have proved inadequate for the current, more complex demands of coordinating a system. A third category of states, illustrated by Michigan, consists of those making initial fact-finding inquiries about the condition of higher education.

These three states undertook an examination of their respective higher education systems in the mid-1980s. Each state has a distinct structure for higher education. Maryland has one major multicampus research university, eight public colleges and universities, 17 community colleges, 23 private colleges and universities, and a number of proprietary schools. Until 1988, the state had four governing boards and a state board for higher education, which served as the coordinating board and postsecondary planning commission. Michigan's nationally recognized research universities include the University of Michigan, Michigan State University, and Wayne State University; it also has four regionally based "general state universities," five regional state colleges, two technical colleges, and 29 community colleges (Commission on the Future 1984). Each four-year college is governed separately, and the three major research universities are autonomous institutions with elected governing boards, as provided for in the state's constitution. In Rhode Island, a single board of regents for all education was altered in 1981 to form a separate board of governors for higher education, with governing authority over the state's three institutions: a research university, an urban public college, and a community college.

The reports reveal circumstances distinct to each state. Maryland had experienced several years of contention among major actors within and without higher education about the role and scope of authority of the statewide coordinating board and about the provision of educational services in Baltimore, the major population center. Because of continuing disagreements within the state about the structure of Maryland's higher education in 1985, Governor Harry Hughes appointed the Commission on Excellence in Higher Education, which raised the following policy questions:

1. What is the most appropriate methodology of determining the correct level, process, and distribution of funding of higher education in the coming decade?
2. Assuming an appropriate methodology of funding, is the state's funding of higher education now at the appropriate level, considering the range of needs and programs as well as the limits of state resources?
3. What incentives could be instituted to encourage and increase cooperation among institutions and segments of the higher education community—both public and private— considering their respective missions?
4. What are the appropriate methods of ensuring accountability for the use of state funds? (Governor's Commission 1986).

A widely shared perception about the commission's report (named after its chairman, Alan Hoblitzell) was that it would elevate the statewide coordinating board to "superboard" status with authority to distribute a lump-sum budget to individual campuses and with authority to approve programs, subject to gubernatorial review, and to merge or to close campuses (Graham 1987). The governance arrangement would remain as it had been with the exception of giving the six state colleges their own boards, rather than having a single governing board for state colleges. The Hoblitzell Commission endorsed "the principle of local institutional governance with strong central oversight at the state level" (Governor's Commission 1986, p. 48). The reactions to centralized authority included supplementary reports from the Black Caucus, which called for more student aid provided more equitably (Maryland Legislative Black Caucus 1987), from campus presidents who advocated creating a local board for each campus but giving a single board of regents strong governing authority, and from the state, which wanted to create a new single authority responsible for all of higher education, with particular attention to improving the delivery of educational services in Baltimore (State Board 1987). The final version enacted in 1988 created the Maryland Higher Education Commission to replace the State Board for Higher Education and provided for consolidation of 11 of Maryland's 13 campuses into an expanded University of Maryland system. The chancellor of the University of Maryland at College Park resigned to take a position in another state (Jaschik 1988c).

In Rhode Island, an external team of consultants conducted a study of governance and organization as a follow-up to the Blue Ribbon Commission to Study the Funding of Public Higher Education in Rhode Island. The team focused on interinstitutional possibilities, including merger of the two senior institutions, and found that the missions of the three institutions were distinctive although not universally understood. Interinstitutional collaboration was already in place, with the potential for more cooperative ventures; therefore, merger should not be pursued as long as enrollments and funding among the institutions were stable. The rationale for merger involved basic policy alternatives (McGuinness et al. 1988).

In proposing to abandon the idea of merger in Rhode Island, the consultants considered the experience of other states in organizing statewide governance and coordinating structures.

A major upheaval of the state's higher education system more often than not does not improve either the structure or state support of higher education.

In many cases the problem is not necessarily that any one element of the system has totally failed or that any single agency or individual is at fault. In fact, the reality is just the opposite; key leaders and boards can show an excellent record of accomplishment. What we observe, however, is that the trust and confidence [that] really make a system work have begun to weaken and most if not all the key partici-

pants—the governor, legislature, presidents, system CEO, board members—share some responsibility for the situation (McGuinness et al. 1988, p. 29).

The team identified the common situational determinants that can lead to problems in statewide structure and governance. First, one or more campus presidents may work out an arrangement in which they can bypass the state board, going directly to either the governor or the state legislature. While such strategies have short-term appeal, the long-term consequences may become divisive if the governor or legislators become involved in interinstitutional conflicts and rivalries and if confidence in higher education in the state generally is undermined. Second, members of state-level governing boards may misinterpret their role: Should they take a state perspective or that of an individual campus? System board members cannot be advocates of single institutions. Third, statewide boards may drift into involvement and even preoccupation with administrative, regulatory, and data-gathering functions, thus sacrificing a statewide perspective and losing credibility with governors, legislators, and institutional leaders. Fourth, problems with the state's higher education system, if left unresolved, can become more intense and may be dealt with in the political arena. This situation may cause a governor or legislative leader to remark, "Until the higher education system can get its own house in order, I'm going to concentrate on other state priorities" (McGuinness et al. 1988, p. 29). Finally, a situation may develop where a major upheaval of the state's higher education system more often than not does not improve either the structure or state support of higher education.

In Michigan, a governor's blue ribbon commission created in 1983 produced a report on new directions for higher education in Michigan in 1984. The commission took a systematic approach to examining higher education in the state, focusing on a core question: How can higher education in Michigan become more affordable and accessible, remain diverse and reduce unnecessary duplication, contribute to the state's economic revitalization, and enhance quality? The commission's final report was written with a substantive focus on three issues—investing in people, focusing on priorities, and supporting economic progress. The report identified problem areas for colleges and universities that were related to each substantive policy issue and made appropriate recommendations for policy. In other words, the commission emphasized programmatic possibilities rather than structural problems at the state level and between the state board and campuses. This approach did not result in a balanced examination of issues, but it does appear that not dwelling on structural concerns and problems made a positive contribution to a focus on policy issues for higher education in the state.

In Michigan, the governor in 1987 appointed a special adviser on the future of higher education "in part as an attempt to establish the degree to which Michigan's higher education system has changed since 1984" (Cole 1988, p. 1). The special adviser worked with "an informal panel of executive and legislative staff," with the staff of professional associations and groups, and with representatives of Michigan's public and private universities. The original commission's 78 recommendations were examined, with emphasis upon the actions and activities of the higher education system that responded to each policy recommendation. Thus, communications were fostered between higher education and the state's leaders. Campuses were encouraged to initiate and create forward momentum in as many areas of concern as possible, and additional state resources were matched with institutional initiatives.

Trustees, Governing Boards, and Multicampus Systems
In view of the size, composition, and influence of governing boards in higher education, it is surprising that trustees and members of governing boards were not often studied systematically until recently. Frequently, governing boards were the topic of criticism and commentaries, but the boards and their respective members remained unanalyzed. The concept of lay trusteeship has been a fundamental yet controversial feature of American higher education (Taylor 1987, p. 7). One recurring theme has been that trustees protect the public interest in higher education by protecting the campus from improper external intrusion as well as ensuring that narrow institutional interests are not served at the expense of legitimate public needs. While some view trustees as persons outside the institution whose legitimacy to govern can be questioned, the role of trustees and governing board members in representing institutional interests in the face of increasing external involvement has become more important. More specifically, trustees are credited with helping to increase access to higher education, choosing campus leadership, promoting academic freedom, encouraging faculty to be

concerned with the entire institution and not with only one department or area, and providing assistance in raising funds and acquiring resources (Taylor 1987).

The demographics of governing boards indicate that, nationwide, governing board members are 85 percent male and 93 percent white; more than 65 percent are 50 years or older (Kohn and Mortimer 1983, p. 33). A study of the public sector found that 73 percent were male, 89 percent white, and 66 percent 50 years or older (Kirkpatrick and Pettit 1984). The public sector appears to have a slightly higher representation of women and minorities. In Illinois, for instance, the number of female trustees was estimated to double in the 10 years from the mid-1970s to the mid-1980s (Petty and Piland 1985).

The literature on trustees and governing boards reflects the degree to which trustees have changed in recent years. One of the better-known references in this area focuses on trustees of private colleges with single chapters devoted to "The Public University" and "The Junior College" (Rauh 1969). That work presaged what was to become a major concern a decade later: "There are few boards of trustees which will not in some fashion feel the horns of this dilemma [conflict between statewide coordination and the autonomy of individual institutions], for coordination is widespread and undoubtedly here to stay" (p. 125).

Selecting trustees

Trustees may be selected by appointment, by election, or by virtue of position. Gubernatorial appointment is the most common form in the public sector, but popular election is practiced among community colleges (local elections in at least 20 states) and in seven major universities in five states (Colorado, Illinois, Michigan, Nebraska, Nevada). Private institutions commonly select their own trustees, often using alumni balloting. Appointment of trustees in public institutions has been described as "a fight over the three p's, prestige, politics, and power," while in private colleges it has been described as "a search for people who possess the three w's, wealth, wit, and wisdom" (Kohn and Mortimer 1983, p. 32). Trustees for private colleges are usually expected to be active in raising funds, but in public colleges, methods of selection "often are steeped in the political culture and tradition of a given state or local community" (p. 32).

The debate over whether or not trustees should be elected

The debate over whether or not trustees should be elected rests largely on beliefs about the process. While proponents of popular election argue that election is more democratic and independent from political patronage, opponents say that potentially excellent trustees will not subject themselves to the time and funds necessary to conduct a campaign. Moreover, election as well as appointment, if it involves a partisan political process, can result in trustees who may be less qualified and less interested in serving as trustees. Wrangling over election or appointment may result in political conflict that carries over to the internal operations of the board. "In this latter instance, neither the best interests of the public nor the institution are served" (Kohn and Mortimer 1983, p. 35).

One might conjecture that elected boards would be more removed from the educational process or that the process of selection would be more imbued with politics. Recent investigations have shown that in the five states where board members are elected, political parties are active in Colorado, Illinois, and Michigan (Gove 1986). The key questions relate to future aspirations of board members and how they function in the position, however. Elected board members tend not to use the position as a stepping stone to political office, primarily because the position on the board lacks visibility (Gove 1986). The extent of visibility appears to be related more to the individual board member's behavior and actions than to board membership, however (Nowlan, Ross, and Schwartz 1984). Another fundamental question relates to the extent to which elected board members help the institution in the political arena with such things as budget requests, economic development, or legislative policy. Little evidence suggests, at least in Illinois, that elected boards make a significant difference in these areas. Rather, it is the "flagship status" of the University of Illinois more than the fact that board members are elected that appears to make a difference (Gove 1985).

In composition, boards of private institutions tend to be larger (the average size is 26) than are those in the public sector (average size nine). A compelling reason for larger boards in private institutions is the necessity for many of them to engage in fund raising on behalf of the institution. Accordingly, the number of trustees representing private institutions outnumber those representing public institutions by 17 to one (Zwingle 1980).

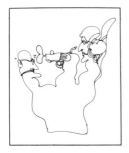

Roles and responsibilities

Several areas of concern emerge from among the many specific duties of board members (Nason 1980, 1984). One set of responsibilities is focused on the chief executive officer of the college. Trustees select the president, support or remove the president, and monitor the president's performance. Some would say the most significant job of a governing board member is the selection of the president. A second role deals with institutional functions, and the issue is whether or not boards should formulate policy or actively engage in administration. Some say that board members should set policy but let administrators manage. The most critical of these management tasks involves finance, ranging from capital finance to tuition pricing to monitoring the operating budget to helping locate additional sources of revenue for the institution. Other institutional functions include overseeing and being involved in formulating campus mission statements; long-range, strategic, or market planning; reviewing specific areas of concern regarding academic programs; and advising the president and top administrative staff or cabinet on special concerns.

A third area of responsibility relates to a role for the board in evaluation, which may encompass evaluating issues and personnel. Evaluating issues relates to the board's having a potential role in assisting with the assessment of policy or legal matters dealing with such matters as civil rights, employment, governmental investigations or reviews, and due process. Evaluating personnel focuses principally on the board's evaluation of the president.

The fourth set of roles for the board pertains to the relationship between the institution and its external constituents. In public colleges and universities, this role includes "enhancing the public image" and "interpreting the community to the campus" (Nason 1980, pp. 42–44). It is in this area, especially in the public sector, where problems emerge. "Boards of trustees often operate too much as conduits for political pressures rather than buffers against it" (Mortimer 1987, p. 26). It is understandable why this situation would arise. Members of public boards are most often appointed by the governor or by the legislature; most members of public boards are chosen with no campus involvement. When the political process is involved, either through party mechanisms or gubernatorial appointment, an opportunity arises for making appointments to serve political ends more than educational ends, resulting in a "fundamental tension between the board's role as a buffer and the way in which approximately 80 percent of the trustees are selected in public institutions" (pp. 30–31).

An area of particular concern, especially in the public sector, is the lack of board members who are minorities. Ample evidence exists that minorities are becoming an increasingly more visible constituent group, as students, as faculty, and as staff. Improving access to minorities and nontraditional students has not been among the most important tasks of board members, as they perceive their duties (Kirkpatrick and Pettit 1984). Board members perceive that their most important tasks are to provide the governor and legislature with reliable data, to articulate higher education's needs to the public, and to ensure quality in academic programs. Tasks of lesser importance include ensuring cost-effectiveness on campuses and balancing the competitive aspirations of various campuses. Minority trustees agree that seeking greater cultural diversity on boards will become a more important goal in the years ahead (*AGB Reports* 1984).

In 1983, an interpretive review of the literature on trustees and academic decision making noted two ideological assumptions present in much of the literature: one in favor of and the other in opposition to "rule by the elites" (Engel and Achola 1983). The authors concluded that additional empirical studies were needed that focus on the link between what boards should do and what they actually do in academic decision making.

System governance

Of particular interest are system-level leadership activities involving system heads as well as members of governing boards. Unlike boards of trustees, which deal with only one institution, governing boards can be responsible for policy affecting numerous campuses. Yet their knowledge of campus matters may be limited (Taylor 1987). Both individual campuses and systems have chief executives as heads, often labeled "president" at the campus level and "chancellor" or "executive director" at the system level. It is the relationship of authority between these two levels of chief executives that defines the character of the system (Pettit 1987). A number of problems involving these chief executives are unique. In some states, both system heads and campus presidents report directly to the governing board, thereby raising the potential for conflict between chief executives. When the system has strong executives, when campus presidents report to the system head, who reports directly to the

TABLE 1

RELATIONSHIP BETWEEN SYSTEM EXECUTIVES AND CAMPUSES

Dimension of Authority	Strong System Authority	Accommodation between System and Campuses	Weak System Authority
Appointment and dismissal of campus presidents	System CEO initiates; board ratifies	System CEO involved; board makes independent decisions	System CEO does not recommend
Reporting patterns	System CEO reports to board; campus CEO reports to system CEO	System and campus CEOs have equal official status; campus CEOs have access to board	System and campus CEOs report directly to board independent of each other
Setting board agendas	System CEO approves campus agenda	System and campus agendas go to board independently	System CEO transmits campus agenda to board
Board presentations	System CEO presents all action items	Campus CEOs present campus agenda to board	Board chair calls on campus CEOs for items
Personnel decisions	System CEO signs off and is final authority	System CEO accepts campus CEOs' recommendations	Campus CEOs' recommendations go to board without system recommendations
Operating budget and requests for appropriations	System CEO approves and submits	System CEO transmits campus requests with independent recommendations	System CEQ transmits to board without recommendations
Academic program review	System initiates and conducts	System may propose; campuses conduct	Campuses initiate and conduct without direction
Contracts for goods and services	System CEO approves or recommends	System CEO transmits to board with recommendations	Contracts approved on campus

TABLE 1 (Continued)
RELATIONSHIP BETWEEN SYSTEM EXECUTIVES
AND CAMPUSES

Dimension of Authority	Strong System Authority	Accommodation between System and Campuses	Weak System Authority
Legislative relations	System CEO conducts	Campuses participate; system CEO coordinates	Campuses conduct own legislative relations without supervision
Recruitment	System CEO has credentials similar to campus CEOs	System CEO likely to have worked in government	System CEO recruited from pool of other state agency heads
Compensation	System CEO paid more than campus CEOs	System CEO similar to campus CEOs	System CEO paid less than campus CEOs
Fund raising	Centralized with one foundation	Single foundation but separate campus accounts	Campuses have own foundations

Source: Pettit 1987, pp. 200–203.

governing board, the system head may suffer from a lack of a campus constituency. These problems can cause a special set of circumstances to arise for a system head that transcends the concerns normally experienced by campus presidents.

Pettit conceptualized the relationship of authority between system executives and campuses using 12 dimensions of authority (see table 1). These relationships range from the strongest system authority to an accommodation between system and campuses to weak system authority with maximum campus autonomy (Pettit 1987, pp. 200–203). It is the system head, more so than campus presidents, who deals directly with the governor and individual legislators. While the external demands on campus presidents are considerable, the external demands on system heads are also significant. A critical issue in the selection of the system head is to select someone who has the ability to function effectively in a role having intense demands involving external actors as well as campus presidents.

Multicampus systems

Since Lee and Bowen published the seminal work on multicampus systems in 1971, relatively little scholarship on the subject has appeared. The 1960s were the "decade of the multiversity—the complex, multipurpose campus—[and] the decade of the multicampus system" (Lee and Bowen 1971, p. 1). Lee and Bowen defined the multicampus university as the coexistence of a number of geographically distinct communities exhibiting four characteristics: more than one four-year campus, the responsibility for a portion of higher education in the state, a systemwide executive with the title of president or chancellor, and an executive not having responsibility for only a single campus. They considered the term "multicampus system" an umbrella term encompassing what others more recently have differentiated as different types of systems. "Flagship campuses" are included in the conceptualization of a multicampus system, but not all multicampus systems have flagship campuses. Flagship campuses across different multicampus systems may have more in common with each other than do multicampus systems with each other, and flagship campuses may have more in common with their counterparts in other multicampus systems than with other campuses within the same system.

Lee and Bowen in 1974 revisited the nine multicampus systems that were the focus of the earlier research, exploring internal campus functions within the context of multicampus governance.

> *The central lesson of the analysis. . .seems to be, therefore, that if multicampus systems are going to make the most of their unique advantages for survival and effectiveness, their flexibility must be considerable and needs to be protected. Such flexibility may be endangered by undue intrusions of state governments, by their own too highly bureaucratized central administration, by authority that is too widely dispersed and too absolute at the campus and department levels, or by the introduction of new coordinating centers with control over institutional procedures* (Lee and Bowen 1975, p. x).

Multicampus systems have considerable influence in higher education because of the numbers they represent. Approximately 48,000 individuals serve on 22,000 governing boards associated with the 3,200 colleges and universities in the United States (Mortimer 1986). About 200 are multicampus boards governing one-third of all campuses and representing about 55 percent of the 12 million students enrolled in higher education (Mortimer 1986). The multicampus system, a creation of the post–World War II period, includes many campuses established after 1960 that operate within multicampus systems (Harcleroad and Ostar 1987). Of the four types of multicampus systems—private multicampus systems, including two systems affiliated with religious denominations and four independent systems, 19 statewide multicampus systems, eight heterogeneous public multicampus systems containing both junior and senior colleges governed by a board with less than statewide jurisdiction, and 38 homogeneous public multicampus systems having less than statewide jurisdiction over junior or senior colleges (Creswell, Roskens, and Henry 1985)—homogeneous public multicampus systems are the most common multicampus structure operating at present.

Grapevine, the monthly research report of state tax appropriations for higher education, contains a dichotomy of multicampus universities and consolidated systems of higher education (Hines 1987). Multicampus universities have three distinguishing characteristics: the oldest and frequently the largest campus as the primary "home" campus, two- or four-year branch campuses or specialized institutions like a medical school, and all campuses governed by a single board, frequently one attached to the primary campus. Consolidated systems include campuses that existed before the system was created. Often located at distances from each other, the campuses are administered separately, but a single governing board was developed after the campuses were created. Usually, this governing board is not connected to the primary campus but often is located in the state capital.

Some noteworthy trends in state support to multicampus universities and consolidated systems have occurred in recent years. Until 1986, multicampus universities showed a slightly stronger rate of gain in state support than consolidated systems of higher education (Hines 1987). In 1986, the rates of gain in the two types of systems were identical, but beginning in 1987 and continuing in 1988, the rates of gain in consolidated sys-

Beginning in 1987 and continuing in 1988, the rates of gain [in state support] in consolidated systems began to outdistance the rates of gain in multicampus universities.

tems began to outdistance the rates of gain in multicampus universities. Some of the reasons for these differences in rate of gain depend on political influence more than on objective factors pertaining to the budget base or revenue patterns (Matsler 1988). A correlation exists between increased institutional visibility because of successful athletic teams and increases in state support (Coughlin and Erekson 1986).

Governors and Higher Education

Governors have always been involved in higher education, but until recently their role has been confined largely to their position as the state's chief executive. During the 1980s, governors emerged as visible, active policy makers with significant influence on higher and postsecondary education. Some former governors served critical roles relative to higher education (Atiyeh 1986; Dreyfus 1982; Newman 1985b; Robb 1982; Winter 1985). One informed observer posited that "within most states, the governor has now become the most important single person in higher education" (Kerr 1985, p. 47).

Governors' involvement in education is not only of recent origin. Early participants included Aycock of North Carolina, Montague and Swanson of Virginia, and Comer of Alabama, who served in the initial years of the 20th century (Krotseng 1987). Even earlier, however, were Governor William Davie of North Carolina, who founded the University of North Carolina in 1789, and Abraham Baldwin, who served as a state legislator and congressman from Georgia and worked for the chartering of the University of Georgia in 1785. Davie and Baldwin envisioned public universities as the capstone of an entire state system of public education with open access to all (Johnson 1987). The most accurate descriptor of such early governors is that of a "builder," a state official who used the power of the office to improve education by constructing new facilities and expanding state appropriations. Twenty governors who served since 1960 worked to advance education, and embraced concepts such as quality and excellence; many had some prior relationship with education before becoming governor. Many were able to obtain significant additional revenue for education, even by raising taxes.

Since midcentury, governors generally have become more involved in higher education, initially in providing leadership as states developed higher education systems, including community and two-year colleges. More recently, governors have become involved in issues of access and quality, system consolidation, and relations between public and private campuses (Zollinger 1985). Another recent issue focuses on states' economic conditions and how higher education might help improve a state's economy, particularly in areas involving technology, industrial development, and job training (Herzik 1985). During the 1970s and in some states during the 1980s, however, the condition of the economy and the status of higher education systems have been uneven and unfavorable. It is during such tenuous times that positive relations with key policy makers, such as governors, can be critical. Governors will have to grapple with seven particularly troublesome issues in the near future: contentious or conflicting relationships between public and private institutions, strained relationships between "the more elite and the less elite institutions" regarding such things as job training and conducting research, funding formulas for higher education, faculty unionization, shifts in the labor market, teacher education, and affirmative action (Kerr 1985, p. 49).

Traditional gubernatorial roles include serving as chief executive, chief budget officer, and chief opinion and political party leader—roles that have direct implications for higher education (Adler and Lane 1985). Chief executives not only appoint members to governing boards and councils but also approve or veto bills affecting higher education passed by state legislatures. Governors have great influence over budget issues. They approve or veto appropriations bills and fiscal legislation, and they have budget bureaus or administrative departments that review operating and capital budgets for higher education. Governors are opinion leaders and leaders of their political party. As such, governors speak for the state, travel throughout the state, and perhaps more than any other public official focus attention and mobilize public opinion on policy issues.

Governors' formal powers
The influence of governors and state legislatures on higher education has increased in recent years. In general, a trend toward increased centralization of authority has occurred in government at both state and federal levels. Governors have increased their powers over the formulation of policy, and the technical capacity of state legislatures has been enhanced. A composite index of governors' formal powers is shown in table 2 (pages 24–25).

One measure of gubernatorial influence is the extent of formal powers over a number of specific areas (Beyle 1983). Bud-

TABLE 2
COMBINED INDEX OF THE FORMAL POWERS OF THE GOVERNORS, 1981

		Tenure Potential	Appointive Powers	Budgetary Powers	Organizational Powers	Veto Powers	Total Index
Very strong	New York	5	5	5	4	5	24
	Hawaii	4	5	5	4	5	23
	Maryland	4	4	5	5	5	23
	Massachusetts	5	5	5	5	3	23
	Minnesota	5	5	5	3	5	23
	New Jersey	4	4	5	5	5	23
	Pennsylvania	4	5	5	4	5	23
	Utah	5	4	5	4	5	23
Strong	California	5	5	5	2	5	22
	Connecticut	5	3	5	4	5	22
	Illinois	5	5	5	2	5	22
	Michigan	5	2	5	5	5	22
	South Dakota	4	3	5	5	5	22
	Wyoming	5	4	5	3	5	22
	Arizona	5	3	5	3	5	21
	Colorado	5	3	5	3	5	21
	Delaware	4	4	5	3	5	21
	Idaho	5	3	5	3	5	21
	Iowa	5	4	5	2	5	21
	Alaska	4	1	5	5	5	20
	Maine	4	4	5	5	2	20
	Montana	5	3	5	4	3	20
	Tennessee	4	4	5	3	4	20
Moderate	Missouri	4	1	5	4	5	19
	Nebraska	4	4	5	1	5	19
	Ohio	4	3	5	2	5	19
	Virginia	3	4	5	4	3	19
	Wisconsin	5	3	5	3	3	19

Florida	4	1	5	3	5	18
Georgia	4	2	5	2	5	18
Kansas	4	2	4	3	5	18
Kentucky	3	4	5	2	4	18
Louisiana	4	4	4	1	5	18
North Dakota	5	1	5	2	5	18
West Virginia	4	3	5	2	4	18
Alabama	4	3	5	1	4	17
Arkansas	2	4	5	2	4	17
New Mexico	3	4	5	2	3	17
Oklahoma	4	2	5	1	5	17
Washington	5	2	5	2	3	17
Indiana	4	5	5	1	1	16
Oregon	4	1	5	3	3	16
Rhode Island	2	4	5	3	2	16
Vermont	2	4	5	3	2	16
Nevada	4	3	5	1	2	15
New Hampshire	2	1	5	4	2	14
North Carolina	4	5	3	2	0	14
Weak Mississippi	3	2	1	1	5	12
Texas	5	1	1	1	3	11
South Carolina	4	1	1	1	3	10
Average score	4.1	3.2	4.7	2.9	4.1	19.0

Scales included Tenure Potential from very strong (four-year term, no restraint on reelection—5 points) to very weak (two-year term, one reelection permitted—1 point); Appointive Powers from very strong (with the governor appointing state officials—5 points) to very weak (appointed by department director, board, legislature, or civil service—1 point—or elected by popular vote—0 points); Budgetary Powers from very strong (governor having full responsibility—5 points) to very weak (governor shares responsibility with another popularly elected official—1 point); Organizational Powers from very strong (5 points) to very weak (1 point), depending on governors' powers to create/abolish offices and to assign purposes, authorities, and duties; and Veto Powers from very strong (item veto plus at least three-fifths of legislature to override—5 points) to weak (no veto of any kind—0 points).

Source: Beyle 1983, pp. 458–59. From Virginia Gray, Herbert Jacob, and Kenneth N. Vines, eds., *Politics in the American States: A Comparative Analysis*, 4th ed. Copyright © 1983 by Virginia Gray, Herbert Jacob, and Kenneth N. Vines. Reprinted by permission of Scott, Foresman and Company.

getary power is the best-known of the formal powers, dealing with whether or not the governor shares budgetary powers with a civil servant or person appointed by someone other than the governor, with the legislature, with someone popularly elected, or with others. Another area involves how long the governor may serve and whether the governor can serve for more than a single term. A third area is the power of appointment, involving the state bureaucracy and agency personnel, including the higher education agency and those who serve on governing boards, coordinating boards, and councils. Governors have organizational powers regarding creating or abolishing offices, conferring organizational status, and providing access to key policy personnel. Veto power pertains to override by a majority of legislators present, by a majority of the entire legislative membership, or by a simple majority.

The extent of a governor's formal powers provides a framework for understanding the role and potential impact of the state's chief executive on higher education. Not all governors are powerful, as measured by formal powers, however. A structurally weak governor in a southern state achieved significant educational reform using a combination of resources, including skills in negotiating and building consensus among interest groups and legislators, demonstrated devotion to achieving reform in education, and shifting the need for educational reform to a high priority in his administration (Kearney 1987).

While the formal powers of governors and leadership skills are among the determinants of the relationship between state government and higher education, a more insightful notion in analyzing this relationship is to view both government and higher education as "semihierarchies." Each entity is a semihierarchy in relation to the other because each entity is only partially subordinate to the other (Zusman 1986). While the characteristics of this relationship vary among the states, one determining factor is whether or not the university has constitutional autonomy. If it does, as in California and Michigan, then the authority of each entity over the other is limited. The university has broad constitutional autonomy over academic decision making and institutional governance, but the legislature has constitutional and budgetary authority. In matters where conflict exists between the two, the authority of each is limited. Compensatory strategies may be adopted to circumvent lack of authority. These strategies include using authority in one area to gain control of another area, redefining issues to place them under another authority, or appealing to authorities, such as the courts (Zusman 1986).

Legislatures and higher education

State legislatures also have been revitalized, beginning in the 1950s (Pound 1986). At midcentury, state legislators were primarily part time, legislatures usually met biennially, and only a handful of states had legislative fiscal staffs. Since then, a 30-year reform movement in state legislatures resulted in a number of changes (Pipho 1988). First, 43 of the 50 state legislatures meet annually, and in the remaining states, legislatures meet in special sessions in the "off years." Second, the job of a state legislator is increasingly full time. While many state legislators hold other positions in business, law, education, or the professions, most find that the demands of the position of a state legislator require nearly a full-time commitment. Third, legislative staffing has changed appreciably in recent years. The traditional way to staff legislatures was to have a bipartisan central legislative council or agency draft bills, do research, and work in committee. Now, however, most legislative committees are staffed on both the majority and minority sides. Legislative leaders have their own staffs, usually of considerable size and expertise, and legislators have personal staffs to handle the demands of their local constituents.

The importance of higher education to governors

Whether or not a governor is disposed to helping higher education or views higher education as a problem requires going beyond formal powers to unobtrusive measures. These measures include the attitude of the governor about higher education; the frequency of communication among the governor, legislative leaders, the head of the state's higher education agency, and university presidents; and whether or not the experience between that governor and higher education has been positive or negative.

One determinant in relationships between governors and higher education is whether or not the governor or gubernatorial candidate has previous experience in higher education or the schools. Charles Robb in Virginia and Thomas Kean in New Jersey, a former teacher, had experience chairing the Education Commission of the States, while one governor in the West was openly critical of higher education and viewed universities as "an ivory-tower society" (Mooney 1987a). More significant than prior experience in education, however, are governors' views about how higher education helped to stimulate the economy, improve job training, and increase research and development.

> *But almost all [candidates] consider higher education to be a subject that now, more than ever before, deserves to be addressed along with such other basic state issues as economic development, prisons, taxes, and highway improvements. The reasons, say those who follow state education policies, have as much to do with regional economies as they do with a general desire among states to improve education* (Mooney 1986, p. 15).

In the 1980s, the confluence of higher education's needs with the needs of many states, especially in areas of economic development and training, resulted in the ascendancy of higher education as a key policy issue. Every indication suggests that this situation will continue. The importance of higher education as a policy issue was confirmed in a 1986 national study involving responses from 32 governors (Gilley and Fulmer 1986). Forty-seven percent of the governors placed education at the top of their agendas, yet governors did not view campus presidents or the higher education associations in Washington, D.C., as their most important sources of information. Rather, they viewed the Education Commission of the States, the National Governors' Association, and their own education aides as more important. In another study, which used interview data from case studies in six states, state-level education leaders were viewed as having the opportunity to influence policy makers, especially if their positions were close to the top of the educational structure, but leaders in education generally did not have as much influence as those within state government. Perhaps one reason why educational leaders had less influence is that governors in more than one-third of the states appointed their own aides for education and higher education (Davis 1988).

The appointment of gubernatorial aides for education and the professionalization of state legislatures indicate that policy decisions are made in a complex and multifaceted arena. Governors are interested in higher education not only because of funding but also because higher education is an appealing policy issue in political campaigns, especially when candidates promise increased funding (Peebles 1986b). Further, higher education is the object of difficult and controversial state policy decisions, especially in states experiencing economic hardships. Such decisions appear to fall into a number of categories. First is the matter of budget reductions for higher education in circumstances of revenue shortfalls, reversions, and recisions. In a number of states, higher education has experienced serious midyear reductions because of revenue shortfalls. Such reductions open up a range of negative issues, including the magnitude of reductions and where and how to reduce operating budgets, about which state and higher education leaders negotiate, often in disagreement (Jaschik 1987f, 1987l; Mooney 1987c). Governing board members, governors, and legislative leaders in a number of states have disagreed publicly about these matters (Jaschik 1987o). While media accounts may exaggerate these issues somewhat, one might speculate whether such disagreements are temporary or whether they will be the cause of longer-term friction that may surface in other places.

A second area of controversy deals with charges of impropriety, grand jury and other investigations, and allegations against higher education officials (Jaschik 1987a). Apart from the issue of guilt or innocence, these actions and allegations bring increased public scrutiny to higher education. Third, instances of conflicts and public argument over selection of CEOs for higher education at the state level and even campus presidencies have increased in both number and intensity (McCain 1986). Some level of discord would be expected over the selection of state agency heads; however, the amount of disagreement and the nature of the conflicts, including disagreements between the governor and the legislature and others involving vocal members of governing boards, bring a new level of tension to higher education at the state level. Oregon is a case in point when the governor asked the chancellor to resign; although the governor does not appoint the chancellor, he and others were influential when finalists for the chancellor's position either withdrew or were rejected by the Board of Higher Education (Blumenstyk 1988). A case at the campus level involved the dismissal of a president in Texas, officially for "philosophical differences" with the board but allegedly for political differences between the governor and the president. The dismissed president commented, "[The governor] didn't like my politics, and he didn't like my friends. . . .The governor denies it, of course, but a former top member of his staff privately confirmed it. 'It was politics, all right,' he told me'' (Hardesty 1988, p. 1).

Whether or not state support of higher education will increase likely will depend on the success of the efforts in the economic sector. The success of reinvigorating the state's economy and higher education in New Jersey is a case in point. When Thomas Kean was elected in 1981, New Jersey's economy was deteriorated and its public sector heavily bureaucratized. The keys in New Jersey's transformation were ''a steady determination and a statewide collaboration involving the governor, higher education officials, business leaders, and legislators'' (Mooney 1987b, p. 20). The state initiated programs involving competitive and challenge grants, targeted research monies to academic fields allied with growth industries, and passed legislation in 1986 giving increased autonomy to state colleges. The legislation on autonomy transferred authority to colleges to set tuition and purchase supplies. Along with efforts to improve quality and implement an assessment program involving students and colleges, state-level higher education leaders aggressively pursued a program to enhance participation by minorities. Thus, one can see collaborative efforts simultaneously on two fronts: the state and higher education joining together to link campuses with economic development, and the joint enhancement of quality and performance, with greater participation of minorities in higher education.

Governors and educational reform

While economic development and higher education captured the interest of governors, the topic of educational reform grew in significance as a critical policy issue. When the governors' 1991 report on education, *Time for Results*, was released in 1986, the chair, Governor Lamar Alexander, pointed out the direction to be followed:

> *The Governors are ready to provide the leadership needed to get results on the hard issues that confront the better schools movement. We are ready to lead the second wave of reform in American public education* (National Governors' Association 1986, p. 2).

Of the seven task forces formed, one dealt directly with higher education: the Task Force on College Quality. It was charged with answering the question, "How much are college students really learning?" Chaired by Governor John Ashcroft of Missouri, the task force examined college assessment of student learning. In 1987, *Results in Education* provided an overview of progress in state policy in each of the seven areas (National Governors' Association 1987b). With regard to college quality, seven states in 1987 were listed as revising or developing role and mission statements for higher education. Progress reports will be issued each year through 1991, when a final report will be published.

Lobbying for Higher Education

Before the 1980s, lobbying for higher education was characterized by passivity and ineffectiveness at the federal level (Brademas 1987; Moynihan 1980), and it was not well understood at the state level (Gove and Carpenter 1977). That situation began to change in the mid-1970s, although accounts of higher education's effective lobbying did not appear in the literature until more recently. At the federal level in the mid-1970s, a politically astute staff was hired at the American Council on Education, and more coordinated activities were initiated involving the "Big Six," the major, federal-level higher education associations. The associations' successful impact was felt with passage of the Education Amendments of 1976, the tax credits and Middle-Income Student Assistance Act of 1978, and the Higher Education Reauthorization Act of 1980 (Bloland 1985). Higher education began to have "a respectable political presence in Washington" (O'Keefe 1985). At the state level, lobbying involved major institutions and higher education systems, although lobbying was not analyzed in any systematic fashion.

In 1980, the White House changed ideologically to a mood favoring deregulation and decentralization and annual federal assaults on student aid, including Pell grants and student loans. Relations between the federal government and higher education became what one editor described as "government by confrontation" (A. Bernstein 1985), and the effects of conservatism on higher education began to be felt. Among these effects were continued governmental attempts to reduce the magnitude of student financial aid, to reduce governmental support for basic research, and to emphasize excellence—not necessarily at the expense of access, despite interpretations to the contrary (Morgan 1983). These developments at the federal level had far-reaching ramifications for the states, including reductions on

In 1980, the White House changed ideologically to a mood favoring deregulation and decentralization and annual federal assaults on student aid.

the campus as a result of the inability to increase state support because federal funds were cut, shifting additional costs to students in the form of higher tuition, and reducing programs because of increased measures to cut costs.

State-level lobbying

Lobbying for higher education at the state level has been more decentralized and more institutionally based than lobbying at the federal level. Higher education associations play a significant role in lobbying at both federal and state levels, but at the state level, associations use the talents and resources of institutions in their quest for resources. A prime example of the effectiveness of a state-level higher education agency is the success of the New England Board of Higher Education in obtaining a three-year competitive grant from the Fund for the Improvement of Post-Secondary Education. The purpose of the grant was to use "informed analysis of comparative data to educate the legislators on the connection between public investment in higher education and economic development" (M. Bernstein 1985). The project informed legislators about higher education and its actual as well as potential role in stimulating economic development in New England. A survey was taken of state legislators about their knowledge and preferences regarding economic development and higher education. Policy briefings were held with legislators in the six New England states, followed by publication of the proceedings of each briefing. Periodic reports were made to a legislative council. The project not only increased awareness of the role that higher education could play in economic development but also created collaborative relations between lawmakers and educators, thus building a foundation for increased opportunities for higher education.

The traditional approach to lobbying has been to confine it to a small number of influential individuals with a strong institutional or community base who, in the interests of their institution or group of institutions, persuade legislators to pass appropriations bills. Increasingly, it is recognized that this traditional approach to lobbying has limited returns. The "new style of lobbying" features broad-based coalitions and relations with potential allies outside higher education. It makes wider use of focused communications targeted toward diverse audiences to increase a state's resources and broaden the budgetary base not simply in narrow self-interest.

Higher education appropriations do not exist in a policy

vacuum. If public colleges and universities are to receive adequate state funding in an era of scarce resources and increasing demands, they must be as concerned about the size of the total revenue pie as they are about the proportion of their individual slice. For any state agency, practicing status quo politics probably means accepting a fixed fraction of a shrinking whole. Public higher education, then, must direct some of its political attention to policies aimed at increasing state revenues (E. Jones 1984, p. 11).

The lobbying process

The literature on lobbying for higher education has grown appreciably since the 1970s. A 1980 review of the literature found a limited number of sources on lobbying at the state level (Hines and Hartmark 1980). Now one can find multiple sources written by higher education officials on the mechanics of lobbying (Angel 1980; Gupta 1985; Kennedy 1981; Martorana and Broomall 1983; Rabineau 1984; Shaw and Brown 1981) as well as essays by lawmakers on how, why, where, and when to lobby (Ford 1980; Heftel 1984; Holmes 1983). These articles are oriented toward involvement: how and where higher education can take the initiative to become more involved with state and federal representatives. This literature does little to answer the more subtle questions of self-interest versus collective interest, however: How are conflicts between and among institutions resolved? Can fundamental differences between public and private campuses be worked out *within* higher education before issues reach a public forum? How will law makers benefit from the additional resources committed to higher education? This latter issue is especially significant in the area of economic development. Increased investment of public funds in higher education toward the goal of increased economic development is predicated on the assumption that there will be a payoff, that economic activity will increase, that the tax base will expand, and that revenue will increase.

A limited number of more detailed cases on state-level lobbying appear in the literature. One case focuses on higher education's reaction to the populist tax-reduction initiatives in California: Proposition 13 in 1978 and Proposition 9 in 1980 (Breunig 1980). In 1978, the passage of Proposition 13 reduced California's property taxes by $7 billion, and in turn the state reduced the budgets of the campuses in the three systems in California. Proposition 9 would have reduced the state personal income tax by an average of 54 percent. The passage of Proposition 13 was the result of a combination of a tax revolt by the public and the inability of higher education to communicate to the public the resulting impact of the reduced budget. The failure of Proposition 9, on the other hand, was largely the result of higher education's organized and effective response and the public's negative reaction to what were characterized as excessive tactics by proponents of tax reduction.

Two other cases include daily chronicles in the lives of lobbyists. One case deals with the approach taken by representatives of the University of Miami in Tallahassee (the Medical School at the university receives an appropriation from the state). The approach involves establishing a physical location in the state capital, creating a telecommunications network with the university, staying abreast of legislative bills daily, and using a complex network of personal connections through the university and in the community (Clarke 1981). Of particular interest are examples of direct connections to the governor (who had resided in Miami), work with statewide associations and organizations, and coalitions with others having similar interests. The other case involves the assistant to the president and lobbyist for Weber State College, who worked in the Utah legislature for passage of an appropriations bill for higher education. Of particular importance are establishing trust with legislators, providing accurate and reliable information, maximizing communications among law makers and educators, and building coalitions (Mooney 1987c).

Another case deals with a successful grass-roots campaign by Dowling College, a small liberal arts college on Long Island, for passage of state legislation to increase Bundy Aid, the state appropriation to private colleges and universities based on the number of degrees granted. Dowling's success came as the result of a carefully organized campaign to mobilize major constituent groups, including college trustees, alumni, faculty, staff, parents of students, local business people, and students (Recer 1980). Of interest is a statement about the "multiplier," the assumption that when elected officials receive a letter, 99 other people probably have similar views.

Finally, *The Chronicle of Higher Education* contains reports about the success in Texas to have state appropriations increased. Lobbying by Texas campuses increased markedly in the state legislature, and higher education was able to be represented by powerful allies external to the academy. Prominent among supporters were the lieutenant governor and business people in the state, who formed a political action committee on behalf of higher education that activated a group called "Grassroots Texas" (Jaschik 1987j). In a series of whistle-stop tours throughout the state, participants talked about "their willingness to pay higher taxes, the problems facing higher education, and the role of colleges in improving the state's economy" (Jaschik 1987j, p. 24). A grass-roots campaign in Illinois to promote an increase in the state income tax also was successful, as judged by legislators, but a tax increase did not pass for the second consecutive year because of the inability of the Republican governor and Democratic legislative leaders to agree on a tax increase and reform of Chicago public schools.

The downside of lobbying

Increased lobbying can lead to a number of problems within higher education and between higher education and its constituents. In 1987, a rift occurred between college presidents and bookstore managers regarding the lobbying of the latter about the unrelated business income portion of the IRS Tax Code. Presidents and their subordinates found themselves on opposite sides of the issue (Jaschik 1987c). Even stronger feelings exist over the question of whether or not higher education should establish political action committees (Wilson 1987). Proponents argue that higher education needs the strength and aggressiveness represented by such committees. Opponents note that PACs are immoral and inappropriate for higher education.

> For us, politics is something to be talked about, even as a reputable academic discipline, but not to be engaged in. . . . Politics is an inescapable part of any human enterprise. When it comes to Washington politics, higher education should either play the game to the full—with integrity, to be sure—or work to change the rules. To play with half a deck is to hide from the realities of a complex society (O'Keefe 1985, p. 13).

Another problem is that higher education officials may have limited impact on governors and legislators. In 1986, a national survey of governors found that governors listen to their own staff aides, the Education Commission of the States, and the National Governors' Association more than they do to campus presidents and to state and federal higher education associations (Gilley and Fulmer 1986).

Still another problem related to lobbying is that it places severe demands on those involved, including chief executive officers. In fact, some have speculated that such stress may be one reason for short-term presidencies. Since 1980, the average tenure for a president of one of the 149 universities associated with the National Association of State Universities and Land-Grant Colleges dropped from 4.6 to 4.2 years (Davis 1988).

Accountability, Autonomy, and Regulation

In the early 1970s, accountability was a watchword for a debate that focused on the responsibility of higher education to public authorities. It occurred following a period when higher education had been criticized because of student protests and campus upheavals. Increased administrative accountability, it was thought, would bring about greater organizational control over dissident students and faculty. At that time, accountability was viewed as a means to achieve greater efficiency and to enhance administrative control. Accountability, to some, had external and internal dimensions (Mortimer 1972). Because of the public nature of colleges and universities as social institutions, they were viewed as needing to be answerable to the public interest through budget and information-reporting mechanisms involving the executive branch and the state legislature.

An examination of the evolving relationship between state government and higher education noted that academic freedom is a fundamental characteristic necessary for effective teaching and learning, protected by substantive autonomy that is the power of an institution to govern itself without outside controls (Berdahl 1971). Substantive autonomy, the freedom to protect the academic core of the institution, deals with who is to be admitted, what is to be taught, and how it would be evaluated. *Procedural autonomy*, in contrast, refers to establishing categories in the budget, conducting required postaudits of appropriated funds, and formulating common definitions of terms viewed as being within the state's interest.

Along with the expansion of higher education in the 1960s and 1970s came regulations dealing with social legislation—employment policies, occupational safety and health concerns, and policies dealing with admissions, accreditation, and finance (Fleming 1978). Proponents of regulation saw higher education as an area where the disenfranchised needed redress in employment, remuneration, and opportunity. Opponents viewed regulation as excessive and intrusive and higher education victimized by external requirements. Analysis of the state laws affecting higher education between 1900 and 1971 showed that these laws increased in number over time but also that more laws increased the flexibility accorded higher education. The conclusion was that there was no tendency for legislatures in four states involved in the study—New Jersey, New Hampshire, Tennessee, and Washington—to intrude into higher education and to restrict institutional autonomy (Fisher 1988b). Accountability was recognized as having multiple facets occurring in different policy domains: systemic accountability dealing with the fundamental purposes of higher education, substantive accountability pertaining to values and norms, programmatic accountability dealing with academic and other programs, procedural accountability dealing with administrative and institutional procedures, and fiduciary accountability pertaining to finance (Hartmark and Hines 1986). The increasing complexity of these regulations caused some to wonder whether the combined effect of procedural controls was beginning to diminish the substantive autonomy needed by institutions (Glenny and Bowen 1977; Mortimer 1987).

One illustration of how state legislatures implemented procedures for accountability is the performance audit, defined as an "assessment of how effectively an activity or organization achieves its goals and objectives. . .a natural extension of fiscal and management audits, going beyond relatively narrow questions about how funds are used to questions about effectiveness" (Floyd 1982, p. 33). Expansion of legislative interest in higher education occurred during the 1960s and 1970s when legislative program evaluation sections were added to the National Conference of State Legislatures and to more than 40 state legislatures (Folger and Berdahl 1988). Legislative audits can involve preaudits, such as examination of authorized proposed expenditures for need and efficiency; process or procedural audits, which focus on internal evaluation processes in determining such things as relevance and effectiveness of a program; and postaudits, which measure the extent to which legislative intent has been achieved. One author concluded that these audits have limited campus autonomy more than achieving desired objectives (Dressel 1980).

In a more positive assessment, the postaudit was consistent with the need to focus on results with selective studies that stress evaluation of outcomes by identifying goals and objectives and measurement indicators (Berdahl 1977). Focused efforts perhaps are better accomplished by institutions themselves through program review; more intensive evaluation of the legislative program has the potential to "collapse of overambition" (Berdahl 1977, p. 61). One conclusion, based on visits to seven states to examine the form and extent of evaluation of state higher education systems, including governing boards and agencies, found that legislative performance audits had a number of limitations (Folger and Berdahl 1988). First, performance audits tend to ignore the broader state system in which higher education functions, thus not capturing some of the most important elements. Second, performance audits tend to focus on the structure of the state higher education agency more than on functional concerns like the effectiveness of planning, evaluation, and allocating resources. A third limitation is that the evaluators may be persons who are inexperienced or unqualified to make judgments about complex and sensitive higher education issues. Fourth, performance audits may be motivated by factors related more to politics than to an objective and comprehensive consideration of all elements involved.

In the 1980s, excessive requirements for accountability began to be viewed as governmental intrusion (Bok 1982). At the same time, it was recognized that government had a legitimate reason for involvement in higher education. The government has three reasons to want to curtail institutional autonomy: Government has a legitimate position because of its major role in funding, universities are a central institution in the life of a nation and must come under some public control, and higher educational institutions are not unique and should legitimately come under some degree of centralized coordination (Winchester 1985).

While some governmental involvement is inevitable and beneficial, governmental intrusion can be inappropriate, dysfunctional, and bureaucratic, ideological, or political in nature (Newman 1987a). Inappropriate bureaucratic intrusion comes from overregulation, such as that in the State University of New York before legislation that restored flexibility to system management. Inappropriate ideological intrusion involves substantive issues dealing with course content and violation of First Amendment freedoms. Ideological intrusion can occur because of actions initiated by universities or their representatives and not necessarily from outside forces. Disallowing free speech through protest and physical intervention are examples. Inappropriate political intrusion occurs when someone in government intercedes in decision making because of political interest. Examples include hiring a trustee or employee through patronage or constructing a building on an improper site. Intrusion may take place "either to secure ends that in themselves are inappropriate or to secure appropriate ends through inappropriate means" (Newman 1987a, pp. 29–30).

How does one strike a balance between institutional autonomy and accountability to the state? "What becomes clear is that the real need is not simply for more autonomy but for a relationship between the university and the state that is constructive for both, built up over a long period of time by careful attention on the part of all parties" (Newman 1987a, p. xiii). The appropriate role for the state in higher education is to protect the public's interest through mechanisms for accountability and to create a climate where institutions of higher education thrive. This climate will be characterized by the qualities of aspiration, tradition, and leadership. Aspiration is the desire and the intent to excell: "to improve quality, to do more research, to attract better students—but within the boundaries of an appropriate mission" (Newman 1987a, p. 90). Tradition involves political culture, including the way in which the state interacts with higher education, develops mutual respect, and supports the achievement of goals. Leadership involves a vision for improving higher education and state government.

These conceptualizations recognize the dynamic interplay between the campus and government. Complete accountability and absolute autonomy are unattainable—and perhaps undesirable. Under complete accountability, the campus would become a state agency subject to controls and procedures affecting other agencies. Complete autonomy, on the other hand, ignores the legitimate interest of public agencies and does not benefit from the positive reform agenda suggested by forces external to higher education.

> *The key issue in governance is not whether colleges and universities are accountable, nor is it whether they can in some mystical fashion be autonomous. Rather the issue is where the line should be drawn between the campus and the state; and, most especially, how can we separate out trivial interference with essential confrontation* (Boyer 1982, p. 4).

One essay noted that higher education had lived in "relative isolation" until midcentury, when the expansion of higher education really began, and "state government took the lead in this expansion" (Carnegie Foundation 1982, p. 37). The governance of higher education became more complex and new layers of decision making were added. The essay cautioned, however, that "to impose suffocating requirements on colleges at a time when flexibility is required is the wrong prescription. . . . The nation's campuses must be given incentives to achieve efficiency in the management of their affairs" (p. 44).

Deregulating higher education

Deregulation is one issue in higher education about which many people agree. While many claim that higher education is overregulated and that there should be less of it, far fewer know what life would be like under deregulation.

> *Why shouldn't universities be administered like state agencies? We do not have good answers to this question. . . . Why should an institution of higher education be treated any differently from any other state agency? . . . Some leaders simply do not know what they would do with more flexibility or autonomy if they had it* (Mortimer 1987, pp. 22–24).

Since the middle of the 20th century, regulation has increased with the expansion of higher education. The theory of regulation rests on the premise that legislatures lack the technical capacity to fulfill their responsibilities without delegating some authority to special bodies that have the necessary expertise in selected areas (Hobbs 1978). One such area is higher education, where governmental controls are likely to increase because of legislative interest in three areas: giving the public an accounting of the large amount of money involved in the support of higher education; bringing political pressure to bear in applying social legislation to problems in institutions; and coordinating higher education to reduce or to avoid duplication of programs (Hobbs 1978). In a number of respects, higher education functions like a regulated industry. The state higher education agency has considerable control over students, institutions, and programs, exercising influence over the mix and distribution of services as well as new offerings of programs and courses and exercising control over changes in technology or procedures, such as setting class size. The state agency influences the production of degrees. It monitors, if not controls, prices charged to consumers. And it influences institutional size (Thompson and Zumeta 1981).

A rationale also exists against regulation, stated by a question about whether quality and accountability are destroying what we want to preserve and assertions that administrators and trustees are smothered with legalities and directives from state and federal governments. Excessive government requirements for information give the illusion, not the reality, of accountability and efficiency. Higher education is infected with "creeping centralization by shifting authority imperceptibly from campus to coordinating agencies to the state house" (Enarson 1980, p. 7). Others have spoken out against government control (Fishbein 1978), noting that relationships among persons, institutions, and government are damaged by preoccupation with procedural and regulatory requirements (Ketter 1978), that the costs exceed the benefits of regulation (Sloan Commission 1980), that higher education has too much rigidity and bureaucracy imposed from without (Callan 1984), and that state regulations and bureaucracy are an impediment to "the improvement of institutional efficiency" (Mingle 1983, p. 5). Yet it is not enough for higher education officials to complain about excessive regulation and expect that legislators will pass laws that facilitate flexibility. Higher education must make its own case for flexibility. It must identify specific areas where additional flexibility in management is needed and what improvements should result (Callan 1984; Mortimer 1987).

While calls for deregulating higher education abound, the methods of deregulation need to move away from global assertions and focus on specific items. A major area of concern is about fiscal controls and pleas by institutions for additional flexibility in management. Five specific areas have been enumerated where flexibility is needed: institutional authority to carry funds forward from one year to the next, to expend excess income, and to invest funds; authority to procure, contract for, and dispose of property, and to determine personnel policy; authority to reallocate funds among categories of appropriation during the budget year; authority to review and to set policy in sensitive areas like purchasing equipment and funding travel; and authority to monitor or hire through position control (Mingle 1983).

A certain amount of control by the state agency over higher education is inevitable, given higher education's size, funding, and links to government. No such thing as total institutional au-

Excessive government requirements for information give the illusion, not the reality, of accountability and efficiency.

tonomy—no external controls over higher education—exists (Dressel 1980), yet in the early 1980s, observers recognized that higher education encountered too much intrusion from government. The state exerts control over higher education in five specific areas: restricting institutional authority to reallocate funds among categories of expenditures during the fiscal year; regulating purchasing, personnel, and capital construction; regulating retention and management of local revenues, including tuition and fees; requiring that unexpended fund balances be returned to the state; and requiring preaudits of institutional operations (Hyatt and Santiago 1984).

Deregulation has occurred in a number of states. Idaho changed its controls over appropriations from a line-item appropriation based on full-time enrollments to a lump-sum appropriation to the governing board for public institutions. Kentucky passed a bill giving individual campuses more flexibility in purchasing, capital construction, real estate acquisition, accounting, auditing, and payroll. In Maryland, a task force appointed by the governor recommended that campuses be given more discretion in using budgeted funds, in providing incentives for external fund raising, and in implementing more streamlined procedures for submission and execution of their budgets. In Connecticut, a new tuition fund gives the University of Connecticut authority to set tuition and to retain revenues from tuition. Based on a study that found that New York State gave SUNY campuses little autonomy in fiscal, personnel, and programmatic areas (Independent Commission 1985), New York passed legislation to increase the flexibility of the state university and to decrease state controls over it.

The effects of deregulation

The effects of deregulation have been documented in the literature. In Colorado, for example, deregulation focused primarily on the process by which higher education institutions were funded. In 1981, the legislature ratified an agreement between its Joint Budget Committee and all public institutions of higher education in the state. Labeled the "Memorandum of Understanding," the agreement transferred responsibility for financial management from the legislature to the institutional governing boards (McCoy 1983). The memorandum set forth four principles: (1) each governing board should have the final authority for setting levels of expenditure for institutions; (2) the level of state appropriations should be based on general fund support per FTE student rather than on line items based on past funding trends; (3) each governing board should set tuition levels for institutions; and (4) each governing board should be able to retain and roll over cash revenues generated within institutions (Tancredo 1984). While the memorandum shifted authority from the legislature to the governing boards in fiscal affairs, a problem resulted between personnel policy and fiscal policy when the state set pay increases for classified staff without increasing appropriations to pay for them. As a result, tuition levels increased rapidly (McCoy 1984).

A project supported by the Fund for the Improvement of Post-Secondary Education and completed at the Education Commission of the States examined incentives for management flexibility and quality in higher education. The resulting *Catalog of Changes* identified broad policy changes that occurred in Colorado and Minnesota and more specific policy changes that occurred in 13 states (Folger and McGuinness 1984). "Institutional operations are most effective when spending decisions are made close to operations, and when officials have the responsibility for managing their own resources" (p. 2). The most common approaches to improving quality have been to provide special funds for improvement in specific areas, such as engineering, science, or libraries; to deemphasize enrollment-driven aid formulas; and to provide special endowments to attract scholars. In the areas pertaining to specific policies, 12 of the 13 examples dealt with program or institutional funding; one was concerned with testing students to help improve students' basic competency in mathematics.

Deregulation is a complex and sensitive area, and additional empirical studies are needed to assess the results on providing more flexibility in management to institutions. J. Fredericks Volkwein has conducted the longest-running research of this topic, examining the effects of regulation and autonomy on a number of different measures of quality, cost, and administrative organization for a population of 86 universities (from the approximately 120 campuses in the Carnegie classification of public research universities in each state, including each of the flagship universities).

First, Volkwein set out to examine the relationships between state oversight and campus costs. Using data on administrative expenditures, administrative salaries, and "administrative elaborateness" (measured by the number of vice presidents and deans), Volkwein found virtually no differences among those

campuses having a high degree of autonomy versus those campuses with heavy oversight by the state. The study did find, however, that less-regulated campuses depended less on state appropriations and were more able to develop alternative sources of revenue, such as grants, contracts, gifts, and endowments (1986b).

Second, Volkwein examined the relationship between academic and financial flexibility and academic quality. Academic quality was measured by five variables: faculty reputational ratings, research funding, and Barron's, Cass and Birnbaum's, and Fiske's ratings of academic and campus quality. Academic flexibility was measured by six variables from the 1982 Carnegie survey, and financial flexibility was comprised of nine items from a 1983 Volkwein survey. Academic quality was found to be correlated with the level of state appropriations and with campus size but not with academic or financial flexibility. Freedom from external academic and financial control, therefore, was not found to be associated with faculty and student quality (1986a).

Following the second study, Volkwein formulated a number of hypotheses to explain the results. Three of the hypotheses were explained in a third study, which investigated the relationship between autonomy and changes in quality of the graduate program, undergraduate selectivity, and external funding (Volkwein 1989). Changes and differences in quality were associated with differences in generosity of state funding and campus size, not with autonomy. These findings held true not only for the total sample of 86 public universities over time, but also for those receiving below-average state support and for those receiving above-average support. Under conditions of financial stringency and of generous support, "campus autonomy has virtually no meaningful association with measures of quality; instead, the sizes and resource bases of public universities appear to hold the keys to quality" (Volkwein 1989).

Finally, Volkwein summarized the literature on the topic and examined the correlates of state regulation and autonomy (1987). He found that state controls were more common in states with a heavy tax burden, a low proportion of school-age children, a stronger state agency for higher education, an effective and well-staffed legislature, and a high proportion of private universities. Autonomy and quality were found to be statistically unrelated because they appear to have different causes. Regulation derives largely from political factors, whereas quality derives mainly from economic factors; "while political factors may be more influential in producing regulation, university quality may be more clearly a result of state investment" (Volkwein 1989).

With reference to Colorado's efforts in strengthening governing boards and improving budget practices, a similar point was made about the importance of funding to campuses in general and about flexibility in particular:

> *The greatest loss of flexibility to institutional managers in recent years has not come from intrusive state controls of an insensitive bureaucracy. The greatest loss of flexibility has come from inadequate funding. If you keep having dollars taken away from you, there's less and less flexibility in your situation* (Callan 1984, p. 7).

Summary

The state higher education agency is in a key position to provide and to facilitate leadership for higher education in the states. No single best way exists to organize a state structure for higher education. What is needed is an understanding of the history and circumstances in a state, the needs of higher education and state government, and the key actors inside and outside higher education who will be involved in determining policy.

Multicampus universities continue to be a major segment of American higher education, representing one-third of the total number of campuses and over half of the total student enrollment nationwide. Trustees and members of governing boards are key policy makers for higher education. More often than not, they speak for higher education in the state. They have the opportunity to buffer higher education from inappropriate intrusion that may be bureaucratic, ideological, or political in nature. Too often, however, governors and legislators are involved in the selection of chancellors and presidents for political rather than educational ends.

Of the many actors and officials whose functions have influence in higher education, none are more important to higher education than governors; in fact, some believe that the governor has become the single most important person in higher education. Lobbying has increased in frequency and intensity and effectiveness in recent years. A newer style of lobbying features building broad-based coalitions, identifying people outside higher education who might be potential allies, engaging in extensive communications, and broadening the budget base not just for higher education but for increased public services in general. Increased lobbying, however, has propelled higher education into a more general political arena, which brings with it increased scrutiny of the academy, heightened role stress for campus presidents, and the potential for alignments that might affect higher education negatively at some future time.

The debate continues about accountability to the public and the need for campus autonomy in higher education. In the 1980s, the form of this issue has been transformed into an argument about intrusion into campus matters. While observers seldom disagree about the disadvantages of intrusion, the critical questions are who is intruding in what area and with what effect? The era of deregulation has affected campuses primarily in new legislation and administrative practices that have increased managerial flexibility, and the actions have had positive effects thus far. While regulation stems largely from political elements, quality derives primarily from economic factors, such as the generosity of state funding and the ability of the institution to develop alternative sources of revenue.

STATE FINANCIAL SUPPORT FOR HIGHER EDUCATION IN TRANSITION

This section discusses three primary topics of concern on state-level financing of higher education: policy issues related to newer developments in the area (tuition pricing, tuition prepayment plans, and student financial aid, for example), the relationship between the states and higher education in economic development, and state support of private colleges and universities.

Newer Developments in State Financing of Higher Education

The financing of higher education has been a continuing concern of state and campus policy makers. At the beginning of the 1980s, finance was a preeminent issue among the 200 policy makers involved in a national survey by the Education Commission of the States (Van de Water 1982). In 1988, the National Task Force on Higher Education and the Public Interest identified finance as a critical issue (Quehl 1988).

The major policy issues in state-level finance of higher education include tuition pricing and student aid, attempts to raise the level of state financial support, incentive funding, links between higher education and economic development, and the relationship between financing and quality.

Price and cost have emerged as serious policy concerns for both campus and governmental leaders. The two issues are related, as the price of tuition is a key to access. Cost is a fundamental issue for state policy makers because state tax appropriations are the major source of funding for public colleges and universities, and appropriations provide the major revenue for state scholarship and loan programs. Rising costs and containing costs now are crucial issues. The field of health care offers a lesson in cost containment:

> What has happened in. . .health care. . .is instructive. For years, hospital and doctor costs went unchecked. Finally, outside agencies—private insurance carriers, the federal government, state governments—effectively commandeered the health care business and imposed strict controls and regulations. A similar fate may await higher education, particularly in the appropriation of public funds (Quehl 1988, p. 11).

Ample evidence suggests public concern about increasing costs in higher education. Demand for tuition prepayment plans has been exceptionally strong in some states (Michigan, for example), agencies outside higher education are increasingly involved as third-party payers in meeting rising costs, and exceedingly high default rates in some loan programs have given the public cause for concern about higher education's being unable to manage costs (Wilson 1988). Cost containment has a positive side (Longanecker 1988). First, states use incremental budget cuts as a way to reduce expenditures, even in midyear. Second, incentive funding is gaining visibility as a way to reward specific outcomes. Third, cost containment is a means of "creative revenue enhancement," which includes increased state funding where possible, increases in tuition, and greater private giving and spending for higher education (Longanecker 1988, p. 2183).

Tuition pricing and student aid

The 1970s, despite the emergence of watchwords like "new depression" and "hard times," was a period when some asked whether decreases in enrollment might well "make the finance of education easier" (Folger 1977). The major intervening variable at the federal level was the election of a more conservative president in 1980, however.

> *During the 1960s and 1970s, the prevailing view was that society benefits most from an educated citizenry—and that government had a responsibility to assure all able citizens an opportunity to attend college. We then saw a period of escalating federal funds for student aid that led to the popularization and democratization of higher education. During the last decade, however, the pendulum has swung in the opposite direction. The prevailing view is that the individual, not society, is chief beneficiary of a higher education. Consequently, there has been a shift in student financial aid away from grants and toward loans* (Quehl 1988, p. 10).

As demand for "selective schools" increased, admissions became more difficult and more attention was directed toward tuition price. Students are sensitive to tuition price, especially in lower-cost schools and among lower-income students (Leslie and Brinkman 1987). At the institutional level, "Not surprisingly, this has enabled the folks who run the elite schools to push their prices up faster than those at the ordinary schools" (Brimelow 1987, p. 144). Some hypothesize that tuition price is sensitive to demand as well as to the availability of student aid and that desirable colleges will charge as high a price as the market will bear. Others argue that tuition price is driven primarily by the level of resources available to an institution. When available resources diminish because of cutbacks in student aid, for instance, then institutions have no alternative but to increase tuition (Atwell and Hauptman 1986; Frances 1985). Campuses have used tuition as a major source of revenue to improve services, enhance quality, and maintain a competitive edge over other institutions (O'Keefe 1986). Empirical research has shown that higher and more rapid tuition increases, especially in the short term, tend to be associated with lower-than-average increases in state appropriations as well as with expenditures in other areas, such as adding support services, promoting economic development, and increasing public service (Wittstruck and Bragg 1988).

Supporting students with financial aid is a major role of government in higher education, especially the federal government, which is responsible for basic grants (Pell grants), campus-based programs, and loans. Government and families have shared the burden of covering most of the cost increases in higher education; students' self-support has decreased in importance (Leslie 1984). Despite threats and attempts to reduce student aid, the volume of student aid has grown every year since 1980, except in 1982–83, when the amount of student aid awarded fell from $18 billion to $16.6 billion (Lanchantin 1986). Over $20 billion currently is awarded in student aid (Evangelauf 1987).

The rate of growth of student aid has increased nearly 25 percent since 1980–81; however, after adjusting for inflation, the rate of increase drops to a 3 percent decline (Lanchantin 1986). State incentive grants increased faster than inflation and more rapidly than all other forms of aid except loans. These rates of growth did not keep pace with cost increases in higher education, however. Costs rose more rapidly than inflation and increased by 26 percent in private universities (adjusted for inflation) and 12 percent in public two-year colleges. The real growth in Pell grants in the 1980s has been in grants to students attending proprietary schools, where the number of grants has virtually doubled. It is also in the proprietary sector, where loan default rates are the highest. After disproportionate growth in loans to students, the share of aid represented by loans has stabilized at about 50 percent. Nearly 80 percent of the total aid awarded in 1975–76 was in grants, however (Lanchantin 1986). In 1984–85, the share of student aid represented by loans surpassed and has continued to surpass the share represented by grants (College Entrance Examination Board 1987). In 1976–77, about one-third of the college graduates had incurred some loan indebtedness; that percentage rose to 43 percent in 1984 (Henderson 1987). Only 2 percent of those who borrowed had debt burdens in excess of $15,000 when they graduated. Average debts for graduates in 1987 were $6,800 in the public sector and $8,680 in private institutions.

Student aid is subject to continuing debate over effectiveness and long-term impact. Proponents of the current approach argue that the student aid system allows for the involvement of the major parties—government, students, institutions, and the private sector—that each of the parties contributes a share toward student aid, that replacing loans with grants, while desirable, is not fiscally realistic and would cost upward of $30 billion annually, and that private investors are able to recover a return on their investment in the current system (Fox 1987). Opponents argue that the present student aid system has three principal weaknesses: Rapidly rising tuition prices have shifted the loan burden away from families to students, causing unreasonable levels of student debt; the roles of state and federal governments are unclear, leaving an imbalanced situation among state appropriations, federal student aid, and tuition; and projected student loan burdens will be excessive (Atwell 1987). The student aid dilemma is fraught with both technical and political problems:

> *The trouble with overhauling the student-aid system is that it is plagued not only by a handful of big and obvious problems but also by dozens of systemic ones—problems that may have less to do with the intent of a law or the adequacy of an appropriation than with the way a bureaucracy is structured, a regulation is written, a form is composed. Congress and the executive branch may intervene from time to time to correct some defect that is simply too gross to ignore. But the underlying flaws in the system are immune to mere tinkering—and tinkering seems to represent the upper limit of what is politically possible at present* (Doyle and Hartle 1986, p. 34).

State appropriations

State governments are the major source of funding for public colleges and universities and a lesser, but important, source of funding for private higher education institutions. They provide substantial support to private colleges and universities through subsidization of state scholarship programs and direct appropriations to private institutions. State governments have a consistent record of appropriating more money to higher education each year, but in rate of gain the recent trend has been downward. During the 1960s, two-year rates of gain were commonly 40 percent or more, but in the 1970s, rates of gain ranged around 20 percent, and in the 1980s, they fell to the teens. A 30-year low of an 11 percent two-year percentage gain occurred in FY 1984 and again in 1988 (Hines 1988b).

Education no longer has the justification of growth in enrollments to support increases in state appropriations.

What do these rates of gain portend for state support of higher education? While the rates of gain are averages for the entire nation, considerable variation has occurred among regions (Hines 1988a). In recent years, the West Coast states and the six New England states exhibited strong support for higher education, while weak state support occurred in the five Great Lakes states and in the South Central states. The West Coast states' strong economy has been reflected in consistent support for higher education, perhaps excepting two years of relatively lower support in California as a result of the effects of Proposition 13 and in the lumber-related industries in the Northwest. The underlying strength in the economy in that part of the nation is related to consumer growth, diverse products, and a demand for higher education services. New England, on the other hand, experienced economic difficulties in the 1970s but by the mid-1980s had experienced economic resurgence. In higher education, this resurgence translated into strong percentages of gain, with Maine and New Hampshire leading the nation in percentage gains in both 1987 and 1988.

The Great Lakes and South Central regions, on the other hand, experienced continued economic difficulties in the 1980s. In higher education, those difficulties resulted in relatively weak support for colleges and universities compared to other regions of the nation. The Great Lakes region, especially in the industrialized areas of Illinois, Indiana, Michigan, and Ohio, has been unable to recover as quickly in moving from smokestack industries to capitalizing on services, technology, and information. Continued depression in the nation's midsection is related to demographics characterized by out-migration, rapidly growing minority populations, and economies dominated by industries like oil in the South Central states, wood in the Northwest, and farming in certain Plains and South Central states.

The principal difference between strong and weak state support of higher education is availability of revenue (Hines 1988b), which is associated closely with tax capacity, and public support for higher education is related directly to the state of the economy (Wittstruck and Bragg 1988). Unlike the federal government, states do not engage in deficit financing; rather, states constantly struggle with the balance between revenues and expenditures. Especially if elementary and secondary education is included, education accounts for the largest expenditure in most states' budgets. In fact, some observers note that in public institutions the real debate is not about tuition costs but about declining revenues (Jaschik 1988d). Education no longer has the justification of growth in enrollments to support increases in state appropriations, however, except for selected states in the Sunbelt. Other services—corrections, mental health, welfare, for example—are experiencing large increases in demand. States with a larger tax capacity and the willingness to levy taxes when necessary tend to be those states making larger commitments to higher education, as measured by state tax support.

While tax capacity and states' willingness to increase support are critical considerations in financing higher education, evidence suggests that the relationship between trends in state appropriations and trends in student enrollments is breaking down (Leslie and Ramey 1986). The traditional relationship—an increase in enrollment brought about an increase in appropriations, especially in states using funding formulas—has weakened in recent years, more because of political factors than because of economic factors. For example, states using formulas and experiencing growing enrollments may be providing smaller increments for increases in enrollments, and states without formulas are not penalizing campuses losing enrollments. The combined effect of these decisions has been to weaken the relationship between enrollments and appropriations.

Given the political winds of the day, the institution that reduces enrollments in a well-publicized quest for quality probably will gain a superior financial position over the college that continues to pursue quantity, unless substantial tuition increases can be sustained or new enrollment-driven revenue sources can be found (Leslie and Ramey 1986, pp. 18–19).

Innovations in state support

Traditionally, states have used one or a combination of three approaches to higher education budgeting (Pickens 1986): providing dollars per student, usually adjusted annually by the cost of living; "incremental financing," whereby states negotiate a final budget with institutions based on such considerations as proposed new programs and special institutional circumstances; and aid formulas, some more complex than others, using historical costs and amounts predicated on such factors as technical programs, minority students, and program mix (institutions with large graduate enrollments have higher unit costs).

Now, however, states are moving away from traditional approaches to budgeting. Increasingly, states' approaches to budgeting, including those not related to budgetary formulas, are changed. Examples of budget innovations not related to formulas include those related to improving quality, such as adjusting formulas for different instructional programs and creating new funding categories for programs like remedial education, faculty development, teacher retraining, student access, or acquisition of research equipment (Caruthers and Marks 1988). States are making these changes for a variety of reasons. Existing demands—not only from higher education, but also from elementary and secondary education and other state services from prisons to motor vehicles—on available state funds have outpaced available revenue. The 1980s have been characterized as a decade of considerable variation in states' support of higher education as a result of wide fluctuations in the states' economic health and their capacity to raise taxes. In some states, worsening economic conditions may require reductions in support of higher education, and when that case occurs, institutions rely more on revenue from student tuition, fund-raising activities of all types, including alumni and corporate giving, and revenue from auxiliary enterprises, sales, and services. While none of these financing devices can substitute for a base budget, their contribution to an institution's overall financial health can make the difference between a moderately optimistic picture and a fiscally bleak one.

States have responded to new fiscal realities with a variety of approaches to funding higher education (D. Jones 1984). Initially, states usually focus on what is termed "the multipurpose component" to reduce or eliminate special-purpose funding for specific programs. In some cases, doing so may mean reduced funding for politically popular programs like engineering or access for minorities. Or states may choose to use multiyear enrollment averages, labeled "buffering," to smooth a precipitous drop in enrollments in a single year. "Decoupling" is another technique: Funding shifts from enrollment to program to remove enrollment as a source of reductions in funding. Another approach is "marginal costing," in which the effect of a decline in enrollments is mitigated by the reduction of fewer resources than would be the case with a linear funding formula that ignores the concept of marginal costs. Still another approach divides costs into fixed and variable, attempting to identify the "core" of the institution as the area of fixed costs that must be maintained.

Finally, an area of increasing importance encompasses measures of outcome, performance criteria, and competitive grants. Two budgetary strategies have emerged that are used to promote excellence and quality in higher education (California Postsecondary Education Commission 1987). One is to link levels of appropriation to measurable outcomes, thus making funding contingent on demonstrated results. This strategy is exemplified by the Tennessee Performance Funding Program, an effort to define performance objectives and to develop measures that are part of the formula budgeting process in Tennessee (Folger 1983). The Tennessee Higher Education Commission uses six criteria to incorporate variables in outcomes into the budgeting process: the percentage of programs eligible for accreditation that are actually granted accreditation, the percentage of programs that complete peer review, the percentage of programs that administer a comprehensive examination to majors, the value added in general education as measured by students' scores on the American College Testing Service's COMP test, demonstrated improvement in campus programs and services as measured by such things as surveys, and implementation of a campuswide plan for improving instruction.

The other funding strategy is oriented toward institutional practices. States set aside funds to encourage desirable institutional behavior in such areas as improvement of academic programs, faculty development, or student services. One example is the creation of a Fund for Excellence in Virginia, in which institutions compete for grants to improve quality in higher education. Between 1984 and 1986, 23 such projects were funded, including nine at community colleges. A specific example is a program to improve students' writing skills through the use of computers.

Another illustration of incentive funding is New Jersey's use of challenge and competitive grants as mechanisms to add incentives to the basic approach to funding higher education, which had been based on a formula (Wallace 1987). Challenge grants were awarded to campuses formulating a multiyear plan to clarify or enhance mission with value-added assessments and broadened computer use, for example. Competitive grants were used to encourage entrepreneurship in such fields as high technology, humanities, foreign languages, and international education. Approximately $40 million was added to the budget over four fiscal years because of the competitive grants.

Another case study in state leadership is Ohio's experience in its funding plans to increase the quality of educational performance (Skinner and Tafel 1986). This multifaceted effort, targeted toward increasing research productivity and enhancing quality in undergraduate instruction, included grants for community colleges, universities, and funds. An institution-based, statewide advisory committee determined excellence, and a competitive process for identifying high-quality academic programs was developed using external reviewers. Nonrenewable enrichment grants of $75,000 to $200,000 were awarded for such things as a tutorial college, materials development, computer purchases, and resource centers.

College savings and prepayment plans

Concerns about rapidly rising college costs and families' ability to pay led, in the mid-1980s, to a number of initiatives designed to encourage families to prepare financially for meeting the costs of college while their children are still young. As tuition prices kept rising faster than inflation, personal savings rates declined more than 50 percent in recent years (Anderson 1988), and families find it difficult to save for college for at least two reasons. First, the existing tax system encourages consumption but discourages saving because interest, dividends, and capital gains are subject to income tax. Second, attractive investment opportunities for families are lacking because existing investments, such as bank accounts, bonds, and certificates of deposit, attempt to keep pace with inflation but do not yield strong returns after taxes.

Currently, a number of colleges have instituted savings plans. In 1988, Illinois initiated tax-exempt zero-coupon bonds. While attractive as a tax shelter, the costs of underwriting were higher than expected, and the state will have to pay supplemental interest payments if the bonds are used as savings for college costs. The convenience and tax advantage of these bonds may be outweighed by the fact that tax-exempt bonds barely have kept up with inflation over the past 50 years (Anderson 1988). New York is considering a Regents College Savings Fund that would be similar to the state-based IRA-type account that New York initiated in the 1970s. Anticipated public costs will be considerable; they include a guaranteed minimum yield of up to 14 percent for low-income savers, deductions from the state income tax, a matching contribution from the state, and exemption from state tax. Kentucky is considering a tax-advantaged savings plan that would provide a higher rate of return than municipal bonds. National legislation was introduced to amend the rules for EE Savings Bonds. If the bonds were to be used for college expenses, taxpayers would be able to avoid tax liability on the accrued interest. Another plan, chartered in New Jersey, is the Collegesure Certificate of Deposit, insured by the FDIC. This instrument pays a return tied to increases in college costs as calculated by the Independent College 500 Index, maintained by the College Board.

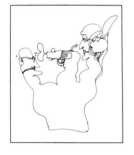

The oldest and best-known of the state tuition prepayment plans is the Michigan Education Trust, initiated in 1986. Those desiring to help finance a child's higher education pay a fixed amount to the state in advance of their child's entering college, with the goal of "prepaying" the value of tuition over the period during which the child is enrolled. The potential growth in the amount of the initial investment is impressive. At Canisius College, for example, parents of a one-year-old child would have paid $7,000 in 1986, which would be redeemable for $128,000 by 2004 (Jaschik 1988b). A major issue in tuition prepayment plans is the potential tax liability, however. In 1988, the IRS issued a private ruling applying only to the Michigan Plan, indicating that interest on the principal would not be subject to federal income tax, but the status of other state plans was uncertain as of mid-1988. A conference of four major associations suggested that parents take a longer-term perspective on investments and consider a wider range of investment options suitable for families' individual circumstances (College Entrance Examination Board 1987).

A number of problems are associated with tuition prepayment plans. One concern is the restriction placed on the use of the funds; another is potentially unattractive returns on the initial investment. While some plans have generous cash-out provisions, others are structured so that one set of institutions may have a competitive advantage over others (Anderson 1988). Another problem is the natural tendency for political promises to outdistance financial reality. Promising low tuition rates at some future point, for instance, may be outweighed by higher-than-anticipated tuition prices, causing underfunded college costs. Still another is that setting tuition levels higher than actual costs may cause prepaid funds to be unable to appreciate rapidly enough. Finally, a general lack of portability in these tuition prepayment plans may prevent students from attending out-of-state colleges, thus narrowing choice.

By the end of 1988, nine states had established prepayment plans, but another 14 states had established tuition savings plans (AASCU 1988). Tuition prepayment plans also have some shortcomings: uncertainty about which agencies will make up the shortfall if investment income does not meet need; the federal tax ruling on Michigan's Education Trust, which subjects a large portion of the investment income to federal tax; and the possibility that prepayment plans may benefit higher-income families. Savings plans under consideration, on the other hand, include a federal savings program allowing parents to purchase U.S. Savings Bonds to use for education, with the interest on the bonds tax free. If states exempt such programs from state income taxes, the savings plans will become that much more attractive.

Higher Education and Economic Development
Of all the policy issues affecting higher education, economic development is one of the most prominent and promising for creating opportunities for growth. "No two issues carry as much combined weight or importance in America today as education and economic development" (National Conference 1986, p. 1).

A review of the literature identified three themes pertaining to higher education and technology: (1) America is perceived as losing ground to other industrial nations; (2) fundamental changes are occurring in the nature of our economic growth; and (3) advanced technology offers future prosperity to higher education (Johnson 1984). A special report of the Carnegie

Foundation for the Advancement of Teaching identified the effectiveness of the United States in the world economy as the most visible new demand currently being placed on higher education (Newman 1985a). The relationship between technology and higher education is viewed in four areas: (1) linking technology with research because of technology's connection to fundamental research; (2) technology transfer as a part of the more general process of innovation; (3) a connection between technology and human resources and an expanded role for colleges and universities; and (4) partnerships and collaborative ventures between higher education and business.

A "common formula," based on states' experiences with ways in which education policies are perceived to enhance economic development, is suggested (Tucker 1986). Faculty salaries at the leading engineering school in the state should be increased. A high-tech research center linked to the leading research university or university consortium should be built. State leaders should enable the research center to become a research park attracting private firms engaged in high-technology activities. The means should be established by which university-produced research results can be communicated to potential users and private entrepreneurs. Relationships between state agencies responsible for employment programs and for vocational education should be encouraged and improved. Low-cost or free vocational training should be offered to firms willing to locate in the state (Tucker 1986, p. 3).

A case study of the contribution of higher education to economic development in the state of Washington identified categories of initiatives that a state might adopt as a strategy for producing benefits from economic development (Zumeta 1987). One category deals with customized job training programs in higher education institutions, although community colleges already are involved in this area. State subsidies can be available for training and retraining employees. A second category is campus-based business "incubators" designed to help small businesses through the early stages of development. Third, research parks could be initiated using public subsidies. Fourth, cooperative programs involving universities and industries—personnel exchanges, student internships, and programs that place academics in industrial settings—could be created, using state subsidies. Fifth, technical and management assistance programs could be based on campus. Finally, technology transfer—stimulating the use of research findings and technological developments from academic institutions to commercially usable products and processes—could involve campus offices of technology transfer. Such campus offices illustrate the relationship between state subsidy and generation of research funds. Offices are established or expanded with state incentive funds, which are used to stimulate more research involving government and industry. An objective is to attain a favorable ratio between research and state funds, often beginning at about a 1:1 ratio, then increasing to two, three, and four to one.

In the literature on reindustrialization, seven critical elements emerge as necessary for economic development: transportation, finance and legal institutions, energy, communication, capital goods and equipment, research and development, and human resources (Beachler 1985). Research, education, and training are essential to successful economic redevelopment—and higher education plays a key role in these areas.

Partnerships between higher education and business

Although interest has been renewed in establishing collaborative arrangements between higher education and business or industry, such arrangements are not of recent origin. In 1862, the Morrill Act enabled the federal government to establish land-grant colleges to improve the economy in agriculture and commerce. More recently, states have implemented a variety of programs that promote partnerships between higher education and business or industry (Spruill 1986). For example, the state of Georgia created the Advanced Technology Development Center as a way to reduce the exodus of graduating engineers from the state. The program provides opportunities for engineering graduates to set up their own enterprises in the state or to join a company based in Georgia. What this and related efforts illustrate is the need for states to focus on the development of their own citizens. Another arrangement is the development of research and technology transfer. Well-known examples are business–higher education enterprises along Route 128 outside Boston and the Ben Franklin Partnership in Pennsylvania. Training in entrepreneurship is another form of partnership in which the state encourages higher education to offer training programs, while the state provides management assistance and tax relief. States act as information brokers to identify industry-related opportunities for research at colleges and universities. Finally, states support start-up operations by providing seed money or venture capital funds. One specific example is to have the state employee pension fund invest a portion of its assets in a business venture.

In research and development, higher education and business/industry have developed collaborative arrangements. Advisory councils comprised of leaders from business and industry can help higher education with decisions on academic programs, fund raising, cultural programs, and athletics. Corporations sponsor academic, cultural, civic, and athletic events. Personnel from business and industry are used to update, evaluate, and revise academic programs. Businesses and industries are a prime source of student aid for scholarships, internships, cooperative education, and outreach programs. Corporations can provide critically needed support for university-based research. Employees can be trained at colleges and universities. And sharing people, equipment, computers, and physical facilities offers the potential for collaboration between higher education and business/industry (American Association of State Colleges and Universities 1987).

A cautionary note must be sounded about moving forward with such relationships, however. First, before establishing these relationships, the participating campus must have established a track record to ensure that institutional policies deal with shared research, applied problem solving, and patents (Doyle and Brisson 1985). Second, both state government and university leaders should candidly assess higher education resources, the needs of business and industry, and the political base of support in the state for collaborative ventures. Third, business and industry must be full partners in the arrangement. If it is decided to go ahead, the unconditional participation of business and industry must deliver more than either could have accomplished alone (American Association of State Colleges and Universities 1987).

Not all colleges and universities will be able to establish relationships with businesses and industries. Institutions exhibit some significant differences in their capability to forge such partnerships. The top universities in amount of resources, demonstrated ability to obtain research dollars, and prestige likely will continue "to monopolize a disproportionate share of prestige and federal research support." In states where higher education systems include both prestigious and "nonelite" campuses, leading institutions will be able to capture a major share of available resources (Slaughter and Silva 1985, p. 301). Universities not in the top echelon are in a more volatile position in their ability to compete for available resources. Future changes in this nonelite, middle-range sector could take any one of a number of directions (Slaughter and Silva 1985). In regions of economic decline, emerging institutions could take over the function and status of established institutions. Prestigious institutions will attempt, however, to maintain their traditional alliances; nonelite institutions may have traditions that could be activated, such as broadening political bases and increasing services. A degree of leveling could occur, with prestigious campuses losing status and lower-status campuses rising to meet opportunities. In addition, shifts in the production of knowledge and changes in the power of disciplinary and professional associations could increase competition between campuses, programs, and individuals for business and industrial opportunities.

Flexibility is the watchword in economic development.

The states' role

Pursuing economic development has its pitfalls. First, one cannot always assume that attracting high-technology industries is the desirable way to stimulate economic development. Some states are not oriented toward high technology. Second, "the high-tech industry of today could be the smokestack industry of tomorrow" (Spruill 1986, p. 13). Flexible plans are needed that recognize the dynamic nature of economic development. Third, bidding wars among localities, states, and regions may be wasteful, despite the attraction of short-term gains for those who obtain a contract. Finally, while reduction of unemployment is one goal of economic development, the causes of unemployment are as varied as the cures.

Flexibility is the watchword in economic development. It follows that changing conditions will be encountered more successfully through links between higher education and business/industry. The states' stimulation of economic development can take a number of different approaches (Osborne 1987), including programs promoting technological innovation, filling gaps in existing capital markets, encouraging the growth of new businesses, helping manufacturing firms keep up with the latest production technologies, moving labor-management relations toward cooperation rather than conflict, stimulating exports, improving education and training, and including the poor in the growth process. Higher education has a potentially major voice in all of these approaches, with the possible exception of providing financial capital.

The National Governors' Association pressed its concerns about economic development with a four-part framework, including developing productive workers, creating efficient workplaces, supporting responsive communities, and implementing the federal action agenda (National Governors' Association 1987a). Noting the connection between education and economic development, Governor Clinton of Arkansas wrote:

> *As important as it is to prepare our people to succeed in a highly competitive world, education alone will not guarantee them opportunities. They also need sound economic policies to provide good jobs. We plainly have both people problems and economic policy problems that must be addressed before our efforts in education can bear full fruit* (National Governors' Association 1987a, p. vi).

Economic development is of fairly recent origin in four-year colleges and universities, but community colleges have long-standing experience in this area (Jaschik 1986a). The current focus is on how and where colleges can assist business and industry rather than on the needs of students who seek additional training. This emphasis has caused both opportunities and concerns. Courses are offered in industrial plants and on site, not simply on college campuses. Many, if not most, of these courses are not offered for credit; thus, they cannot be applied toward degrees. As a result, state aid for such purposes may be lessened—or nonexistent. Solutions to this dilemma have included consideration of changing state aid formulas for community colleges to encourage economic development. Additionally, some colleges and even systems have expanded institutional missions to include economic development. New relationships are being formed between governing boards and agencies dealing directly with economic development.

Effectiveness of economic development efforts
The desire for economic development and the opportunities for collaborative relationships with higher education hold promise to enhance budgets, personnel, and programs for higher education in the foreseeable future. Risks are inherent in these opportunities, however. Gains in one area of expansion in an era of "level funding" and stable budgets may lead to reductions and cutbacks in other, "softer" areas of the institution's budget (Cordes 1987). These areas might include low-enrollment or

high-cost programs, programs experiencing temporary difficulties, or personnel who are not directly connected to activities that generate enrollment.

A fine line exists between training personnel for industry and following the institution's basic mission. State support of economic development has been noticeable in smaller four-year colleges and in community colleges working with small businesses. A match appears to have been made between these institutions and small businesses. Jobs are created at a significantly higher rate in small businesses than in larger corporations, and with help from campuses, small businesses can expand their efforts. Despite this encouraging trend, problems occur when business activity causes unfair competition among local firms, a situation that has caused friction in a number of communities and has led to legislative action in Illinois, Louisiana, Ohio, and Pennsylvania (Jaschik 1986b). Additionally, issues of autonomy and freedom involving the institution and the corporate interest off campus may arise. In such instances, preservation of what is perceived to be autonomy may jeopardize linkages and future opportunities with businesses and industries. While such situations are the exception to date, the potential for their occurring is ever present.

Two additional problems with the complexities of higher education's role in economic development deal with side effects and measuring effectiveness. Economic development involves activities that can generate side effects, such as "a fair amount of boosterism and hype" (Jaschik 1987m, p. 19). Creating jobs, reducing unemployment, putting people back to work, building new companies or rebuilding old ones, and stimulating economic activity offer politicians considerable grist for their mills. A second problem has to do with measuring the effectiveness of economic development. While one way to measure effectiveness is the number of new jobs created, the number of new jobs may not be the most accurate indicator of success, especially in situations where jobs are created over a long period of time or in situations where the creation of jobs is neither the goal nor a representative way to measure the goal. By the same token, the lack of new jobs may not indicate ineffective programs, but may rather be the result of the inability or the unwillingness of a business to use the innovation.

The issue of effectiveness presents a continuing concern for accountability involving higher education and the state. With substantial investment of state funds in economic development,

an accounting will likely be necessary, which concerns some
observers:

> *In each state, politicians, professors, and entrepreneurs have
> visions of creating a new Silicon Valley with their efforts—
> which range from additional financing for promising re-
> search, to tax breaks and cheap land for businesses willing
> to locate in the state, to quick and inexpensive job training
> programs for workers. The programs seem to provide some-
> thing for everyone. Political leaders believe the efforts will
> spawn or attract new industries and create new jobs. Indus-
> tries benefit from concentrated research programs that many
> corporations cannot afford to sponsor on their own. Univer-
> sities receive money from both state government and business
> to bolster their research capacities and gain flattering atten-
> tion from state policy makers and industrialists. Increasingly,
> however, questions are being asked about the wisdom of
> some of the economic development efforts* (Jaschik 1986c,
> p. 1).

A case of success
Identifying individual examples of effective economic development runs the risk of simplification or overgeneralization.
Nonetheless, it may be instructive to examine one long-
standing success story in economic development—the Ben
Franklin Partnership in Pennsylvania. In the late 1970s, Pennsylvania recognized that it had lost 175,000 manufacturing
jobs in that decade. It also recognized that higher education
was one of its most promising assets. Pennsylvania is one of
the top three states in the United States in the number of gradu-
ated engineers. It also has four universities among the top 50
graduate research universities nationwide. Passed by the Pennsylvania legislature in 1982, the Ben Franklin Partnership offers
challenge grants to university-based projects funded by businesses. The partnership is operated through advanced technology centers in four areas of the state. Each center is affiliated
with a major university or universities. In its initial 42 months
of operation, the centers generated 4,530 new jobs and 369
new firms (Jaschik 1987m). In its first four years, the program
attracted $61.4 million in private venture capital (Osborne
1987). While observers disagree about the number of jobs actually created and the extent to which these jobs provide an ac-

curate estimate of the program's success, the partnership
appears to be recognized as a model program:

> It is comprehensive; it is decentralized; it catalyzes signifi-
> cant private investment in important economic activities; and
> it has mobilized major local players in new ways. It is also
> focused on important targets: the commercialization of re-
> search, transfer of technology from academia to industry, the
> generation of venture capital, the birth of new firms, and the
> integration of advanced technology into mature industries.
> Its continued success will depend upon the state board's
> ability to resist the constant pressure from the universities to
> use the money for basic research, new buildings, and the
> like (Osborne 1987, p. 33).

Five principles appear to be related to successful economic
development:

1. State governments are most successful when they take
   time to analyze the regional economy thoroughly before
   moving ahead.
2. The fundamental goal of government should be to change
   the patterns of investment by the private sector, not to
   substitute public for private investment.
3. The task of building local capacity and mobilizing local
   actors is critical.
4. Government should create comprehensive but decentralized development institutions.
5. Economic development programs should not be static
   (Osborne 1987).

State Support of Private Institutions
Private colleges and universities[1] represent just over one-half of
the total number of higher education institutions nationwide,
and they enroll about one-fifth of the total number of students
in college (Carnegie Council 1976)—and the figures are still
accurate more than a decade later (U.S. Department of Education 1987). The Carnegie Council took a positive view about
the advantages of a viable private sector: that larger amounts of

1. The term "private" is used rather than independent or nonprofit, and the
term "public" is used rather than government sponsored. Proprietary institutions are not included in private institutions in this report.

public assistance would be needed in the future, that private institutions need to be involved in planning and coordination of statewide higher education, and that "state systems [should] be planned as a whole" (Carnegie Council 1976, p. 9). The private sector has been valued for a number of reasons: independence of governance, diversity, long-standing traditions, devotion to liberal learning, standards of academic freedom, attention to the individual student, contributions to local cultural life, provision of student access, and competition with the public sector.

One of the fundamental attributes of American higher education is having what has been termed an "extraordinarily large" private sector compared to the other developed nations of the world (Levy 1982). The primary characteristics of the private sector include institutions' diversity in size, location, and academic programs. Private colleges offer students a broader choice of institutions and provide competition with public colleges in values such as quality. These colleges have achieved considerable success in attaining campus autonomy (Zumeta and Green 1987). Private colleges account for 96 percent of all liberal arts colleges identified by the Carnegie Foundation for the Advancement of Teaching in 1987 (Wilensky 1988). These considerations, along with the historic strength of the private sector in American higher education, prompted an identification of "cogent reasons for developing a study of public policy toward private colleges and universities": that retrenchment, possibly severe, would face higher education in the 1980s or beyond and that institutional contraction should not take place only in one sector of higher education; that the higher education marketplace could not be relied upon to direct resources in the best possible way because of a multitude of subsidies and government interferences; that the capital investment, already in place in the private sector, argued for not expanding the public sector without at least exploring the options involving the private sector; and that more than 40 states already had public policies for the financial support of private colleges (Breneman and Finn 1978, p. 7).

More recently, public/private relations as an issue of concern (Gardner, Atwell, and Berdahl 1985; Mooney 1987d; Peebles 1985b) led the Association of Governing Boards of Universities and Colleges to sponsor a national examination of the problem by generating case studies in Pennsylvania, Illinois, Maryland, North Carolina, and New York. They ranged from what Berdahl described as "most cordial" to "least cordial" relations between the public and private sectors, and Berdahl identified a number of intersector issues, including increased competition for students, especially in states having serious problems with enrollment, competition for state dollars in some states, and increased desire by both private and public institutions for private giving and philanthropic support. While public/private relations in these five states ranged from "excellent" to "openly hostile," the intersector relationship was strained seriously only in New York. Yet the case study noted that a number of efforts were under way to effect a possible rapprochement between the sectors in New York. More recently, representatives of the private sector in New York, as well as in other states, appeared to be taking initiatives to improve relations between the public and private sectors (Mooney 1987d).

Sources of financial support

Tuition and voluntary giving are revenue sources of particular importance to private institutions; tuition is the most important source of revenue for private colleges and universities. In 1984–85, tuition accounted for 39 percent of the revenue in private colleges and universities but only 15 percent in public institutions (Wilensky 1988). Tuition price is significantly higher in most (but not all) private institutions than in public institutions. Yet reliance on tuition varies considerably by the type of institution. In the mid-1970s, for instance, tuition revenue accounted for 27 percent of educational and general revenue in leading private research universities, whereas the proportion was 77 percent in private comprehensive colleges and universities.

Voluntary giving is one of the most important sources of revenue for private colleges and universities, and it is rapidly increasing in importance as a source of revenue in the public sector. The private sector obtains about 14 percent of its educational income from philanthropy, with considerable variability among different types of institutions. Some private two-year colleges may derive one-fourth of their operating support from private giving (Breneman and Finn 1978). Of the total giving to private institutions, including capital bequests, about half comes from individuals, the remainder from foundations, corporations, religious groups, and other sources.

Other sources of revenue include tax exemption, federal support, and state aid. Tax exemption is a significant source of

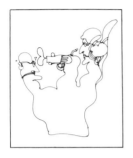

revenue in private and public institutions. Exemption from state and local property taxes is an important subsidy to educational institutions. It has been estimated that the potential tax liability for the private sector alone would have been over $200 million in 1973–74 and certainly would be much higher today (Breneman and Finn 1978).

Federal support to higher education generally includes student aid, research and development, and categorical grants and contracts. By far the largest proportion of federal aid goes to students in the form of Pell grants, and it is in this particular area where many of the concerns of the 1980s have been focused. Each year since 1981, attempts have been made to reduce the amount of federal student aid. While lobbying by the higher education community and others have reduced what otherwise would have been larger cuts, the federal share in supporting higher education has diminished in recent years.

State aid to the private sector includes aid that goes directly to students and to institutions. In the private sector, student aid is the primary means of channeling state funds to institutions, while in the public sector institutional appropriations are the primary form of state support (Breneman and Finn 1978). Student aid encompasses a number of different types and specific programs. Some state student aid is designed only for the private sector, other state student aid can be used at any institution in the state, and still other state student aid is portable and can be taken to institutions in other states. Some form of state student aid is available to the private sector in all states except Nevada and Wyoming (Lapovsky and Allard 1986). Varying types of specific aid programs are available: aid to minority and disadvantaged students (nine states), loans (20 states), state work study programs (five states), nonneed academic scholarships (19 states), and categorical grants to students (43 states) (Gregory 1984). Clearly, tuition grants based on need are the most common and widely available form of state student aid. State institutional aid to private colleges and universities can include several specific types: 19 states (in 1982) had contracts for educational services available to private institutions, direct grants to students in private colleges were available in 20 states, and funds became available from the sale of bonds or capital construction in 19 states (Gregory 1984).

Political influence of the private sector
One of the reasons for the considerable amount of student assistance in the private sector is the influence of private colleges and universities in state capitals. In some states, leadership of the private sector has been an effective presence in the state legislature (Gardner, Atwell, and Berdahl 1985) for many reasons. Graduates of private colleges, universities, and professional schools, particularly law schools, commonly are elected to legislative positions and work on significant committees. In other states, the size of the private sector results in a visible presence in the legislature. Enrollment in the private sector varies across states, however. For example, one-third or more of all higher education enrollments in Massachusetts, Rhode Island, New Hampshire, New York, Vermont, Pennsylvania, Connecticut, and Utah is represented by the private sector (Carnegie Council 1976), but in 25 states, 15 percent or less of the state's higher education enrollment is in the private sector.

In other situations, private colleges and universities have been aggressive and effective at mobilizing grass-roots support in local communities (Recer 1980; Troxler and Jarrell 1984). Despite the pleas by the private sector for increased support from public as well as private sources, the private sector has shown resilience in recent years. While 62 private colleges closed from 1976 to 1985 and no public institutions closed during that period, the number of private institutions increased slightly, from 1,569 in 1980 to 1,597 in 1985, and no change occurred in the number of public institutions (1,493) during the same period (U.S. Department of Education 1987). Historically, private institutions have relied on their own capacities for fund raising and donations from alumni and activate networks to increase their presence in state capitals on other issues where they needed their point of view represented. Finally, liberal arts colleges, well represented by the private sector and numerous in many states, tend to become involved in local community affairs and to have locally based networks that reach beyond alumni and parents of students.

Empirical analysis of the private sector
A multiyear national study of the relationships between state policies and private higher education undertaken by the Higher Education Research Institute at UCLA examined the effects of state policies on the private sector, changes in enrollment in the private sector, and a series of financial variables. The research

included case studies in California, Illinois, Indiana, New York, and Texas as well as a survey of state association executives in the private sector (responses were received from 19 states). From 1970 to 1975, state spending on student aid was associated positively at a modest level with enrollment in the private sector, and direct institutional aid had no significant relationship to enrollment in the private sector. No relationships involving either student aid or institutional aid were found for 1975 to 1980, indicating that by the late 1970s the fiscal situation was deteriorating somewhat in the private sector.

The literature commonly contains hypotheses about an alleged positive relationship between increases in student aid and tuition increases. Do institutions in fact use the increased availability of student aid as a rationale for increasing tuition (Brimelow 1987)? Some researchers found no relationship between rate of change in student funding and rate of change in average tuition at private colleges and universities. In fact, they found some negative relationships in more specific institutional subgroups during 1973 to 1982, indicating that the availability of aid may actually moderate tuition increases (Zumeta and Green 1987).

Data from both the survey and case studies in this research indicate that fiscal difficulties and reductions in the early 1980s did negatively affect private institutions "financially, academically, and probably in terms of the socioeconomic mix of their student bodies" (p. 34). Study of the relationship between the public and private sectors indicated that more rapid increases in tuition in public institutions appeared to help enrollment in the private sector, indicating that students are sensitive to tuition pricing, especially in less selective institutions.

At least on the surface, the private sector fared "considerably well" from the 1970s to the 1980s, as indicated by enrollments in the private sector (Zumeta and Green 1987). Yet in the 1980s, increasing signs indicated that private colleges and universities were suffering under the fiscal strain of cutbacks in federal student aid. While the effects of increased tuition in the public sector likely have a positive effect on enrollments in the private sector, at least in some institutions, the effects on the private sector of public policy decisions in other areas may be more symbolic than substantive. "Though it is virtually impossible to prove definitively, . . . the direct effects of public-sector program competition have been considerably less than the screams of pain from private campus interests might indicate" (p. 38).

Policy and political differences will continue between public and private sectors, becoming more evident and producing more conflicts in states with historically larger enrollments in the private sector. It may well be in the interests of both public and private sectors to discover the areas where cooperative relationships can exist.

A final balance that we have kept through most of our history is the balance between public and private sectors. This accepted difference is unique to these United States because Americans do not see the two sectors as different. We, the professionals, are conscious of which college is public and which is private, but our fellow citizens really look on us as one single system. Not only does the public not see us as separate, but the Congress increasingly refuses to also. All together we provide a cluster of services under different roofs but, like medicine or law, as one national system. The moment anybody starts to see us as two warring parties, we start to paralyze our public as well as all legislative bodies (Healy 1984, p. 10).

Summary

In state finance of higher education, the 1980s have been a period of increasing tuition prices in both private and public schools and a relatively flat pattern of state tax support in most states. During the 1980s, sources of revenue for higher education have diversified, including state-level systems of competitive and challenge grants. Those states experiencing declining revenues because of lagging economies and inadequate tax systems are finding that they are unable to keep up with the demands of colleges for greater levels of support. Those institutions that are responding to the challenge of meeting state needs are finding, however, that they are able to obtain "new money" for such efforts. Because not all institutions can respond in this manner, campuses may become differentiated into "the haves," with adequate funds for new initiatives, and "the have nots," without sufficient resources to respond to such opportunities.

Economic development has attained prominence in higher education. Its ascendancy as an issue of major concern relates to perceptions about America's losing its competitive edge to other nations, changes in the nature of our economic growth, and specific opportunities for growth in higher education. Economic development involves risks: In an era of level funding, new money for economic development may mean reductions in other areas.

In some states, support of the private sector is a major policy issue. States have recognized the value of private colleges and universities. Especially in those states with sizable private sectors, government has responded with programs of institutional and student support. While the viability of the private sector is indicated by slight growth in the number of institutions, the sensitivity of state leaders to the needs of the private sector will continue to be an area of major concern.

CURRENT STATE/CAMPUS POLICY ISSUES

This section discusses four policy issues illustrating relationships between state government and higher education: higher education and reform, minorities in higher education, academic program review, and the assessment of outcomes.

Higher Education and Reform

Reform is change of a basic or structural nature, as opposed to innovation, which is smaller in magnitude and more modest. Reform has been defined as "planned change in higher education" (Altbach 1980). It was seriously attempted during the 1960s, but research universities especially remained essentially conservative (Kerr 1982). The current wave of educational reform is different, however, in at least three respects. First, it was caused by the advent of fundamental questioning about higher education by strong external forces, such as governors, legislators, and civic leaders (Finn 1984a). In contrast, attempts at reform in the 1960s were precipitated by students' reactions to events occurring outside higher education. Second, current reform is broad based and involves constituents, especially those external to the academy. Third, current reform is linked with issues in the larger society—economic development, the improvement of quality, and raising productivity (Newman 1987b).

The recent attention to defining mission, clarifying goals, and implementing strategic plans is designed to establish a link between higher education and the larger society. While excellence and improved quality are common themes in educational reform, varying approaches can be used to attain those goals (see table 3, p. 74). Table 3 identifies six approaches to excellence: political economy, productivity, value-added measures, producer-consumer quality, content, and an eclectic approach (Morgan and Mitchell 1985).

Analyses of reform in a number of states help to explain the nature of the reform movement. Fifteen state studies of higher education found that six areas of universal concern exist: quality, mission and function, efficiency, governance, financial support, and the relationship between higher education and economic growth (Mangieri and Arnn 1986). While quality has been a continuous concern, states define it in different ways: Some link quality to student outcomes, some to improvement in the state's economy, some to academic excellence, and some to enhancing quality as a result of unifying the state's higher education system. Mission relates to clarifying purpose and to

> *The recent attention to defining mission, clarifying goals, and implementing strategic plans is designed to establish a link between higher education and the larger society.*

TABLE 3
SIX PERSPECTIVES ON EDUCATIONAL EXCELLENCE

Perspective	Short Definition	Representative Reports on Excellence
Political economy approach	Excellence is measured by how well schools and colleges support and enhance the political and economic strength of the nation.	Business–Higher Education Forum, *America's Competitive Challenge* Task Force on Education for Economic Growth, *Action for Excellence*
Productivity approach	Excellence is measured by how efficiently schools and colleges convert inputs into outputs.	National Science Board Commission on Precollege Education, *Educating Americans for the 21st Century*
Value-added approach	Excellence is measured by how well schools and colleges enhance individual development.	Southern Regional Education Board, *Meeting the Needs for Quality in the South*
Producer-consumer quality approach	Excellence is determined by the quality of producers (teachers) and consumers (students).	John Goodlad, *A Place Called School* Theodore Sizer, *Horace's Compromise*
Content approach	Excellence is judged by the quality and scope of the curriculum.	Mortimer Adler, *The Paideia Proposal* John Goodlad, *A Place Called School* The College Board, *Academic Preparation for College*
Eclectic approach	Excellence is evaluated on a variety of dimensions, including efficiency, effectiveness, and characteristics of participants.	Ernest Boyer, *High School: A Report on Secondary Education* National Commission on Excellence in Education, *A Nation at Risk*

Source: Morgan and Mitchell 1985, p. 313.

increasing access to institutions. One perception of efficiency is the elimination of duplicate programs. Governance refers to the state-level structure for higher education, with two trends emerging: states' consideration of a single statewide governing structure and a stronger role for state-level leadership agencies. Funding involves consideration of needs instead of simply applying budgetary formulas, linking programs with the budget, and relating the funding of higher education to the fiscal capacity of the state.

An analysis of six statewide reports on higher education calls attention to areas of common concern—program review, finance, and quality initiatives (DiBiasio 1986). An analysis of the reform movement in higher education speculates about reasons for the current emphasis on excellence (Mitchell 1987). One interpretation is that striving toward excellence is a natural response to unfulfilled expectations of higher education and the fact that more people are having fewer children, thus changing the political base for education. Another view suggests that reform is necessary as the economy adjusts to new demands and shifts from an aged industrial economy to a service-oriented economy. A third interpretation posits that reform serves as a device for promoting political careers.

Reforming structures of state governance

Reforming governance by altering or changing statewide structures for higher education is a recurring theme in the literature. The assumption is that structural change will establish the mechanism for change in other areas, such as finance, program, and personnel. More often than not, this assumption does not hold true, however. "There's a temptation to tinker with the structure instead of addressing those other issues, and states that change their systems for such reasons may find both their governance and the underlying problems of the system unresolved" (Berdahl, quoted in Jaschik 1987d, p. 29).

DiBiasio's analysis of reform in higher education in six states discovered that a common theme was the issue of centralization/decentralization (1986). Interest in centralization stemmed from concerns about economic development and improving quality and the assumed advantage of centralizing and coordinating those activities at the state level. At the same time, a move toward decentralization came from a desire to give state higher education systems more flexibility and more managerial prerogatives on campus.

While concerns tend to be specific to a state and proposed solutions need to be oriented to particular needs, some thematic continuities in structural changes have been made at the state level in higher education in recent years. Five such themes have been identified: recognition of the duplication of high-cost graduate programs, interinstitutional conflict within a geographic area, intense institutional lobbying, proposals affecting the status of isolated and small institutions, and a sense that the higher education structure has been ineffective in addressing policy issues (McGuinness 1986).

Maximizing a limited resource base is a policy concern of recent origin, but it is receiving increased attention in a number of states. A sense persists that resources are being spread over too many institutions without attention to quality, distinctiveness, and what is termed "mission differentiation," especially in the public sector. A number of states are actively discussing downsizing higher education, because doing so presents one solution to the problem of insufficient resources and excess institutional demand. Another avenue for expressing similar concerns pertains to efficiency and program review. One way to conserve resources is to eliminate duplicate programs, especially in low-enrollment or high-cost areas. Such reductions would make campuses less duplicative and more distinctive and would reduce demands for resources on the state. Closing institutions and entire programs was unthinkable at one time for political reasons, especially in the public sector (Mingle and Associates 1981), but increasingly, "while [a state] would not recommend closings at this time, it would not want to give comfort to those who think that closings may not be necessary in the future" (Mangieri and Arnn 1986, pp. 37–38).

In many cases, restructuring governance will not offer the solution to the state's problems. "The number one misleading point of view advanced by governors, legislators, and higher education leaders is that governance is the solution to their problems" (McGuinness, quoted in Jaschik 1987d, p. 28). Rather, a state needs to learn from what other states have done and apply reasoned solutions to state-specific problems:

- Have a vision of the future of higher education in the state and a clear definition of the obstacles to achieving that vision, whether they be leadership, resources, governance, or other problems.

- See organizational structure and reorganization as means to other policy goals rather than ends in themselves.
- Examine the total process of higher education policy, not just formal structure.
- Recognize that no perfect system of higher education or no single preferred model of structure and organization exists (McGuinness 1986).

Key role for governors

Many actors have legitimate and important roles in reform of higher education, but governors have emerged as the catalysts in the current effort. They are uniquely situated at the nexus of so many forces impinging on higher education. As such, governors are key initiators in much of the effort, which is more than a fad and appears to be "a bona fide populist reform movement" (Finn 1984b, p. 17).

Educational policy making has become more political than technical. It is clear that the atmosphere has shifted and is now one in which state and federal political policy makers feel that education is too important to be left solely to the educators (Peebles 1985a, p. 10).

Governors tend to focus on results, an orientation that is an excellent match for states to concentrate on economic development and creation of jobs. In a sense, this time is ideal for bringing the link between education and politics into focus, perhaps with resulting benefits for higher education. When political leaders deal with education, they are expressing their values in terms of choices about resources. Generating and allocating resources brings the political process into view (Brademas 1987). As chief executives, governors now serve as a link between politics and education. This link cannot be ignored, because if educators talk only to themselves, educational reform will be short-lived. It is the political leader who will transform the reform of education into public policy (Phillips 1985).

The states' interest in teacher education

The involvement of higher education in teacher training is multifaceted, as is the more general concern about education at all levels, including the public schools. Higher education provides preservice training for teachers and administrators, in-service training on campus and in the schools, supervision for prospective teachers, and research and scholarship involving schools. Of central concern to colleges and universities is the quality of the classroom teacher. Education will be only as effective as the teachers themselves (Magrath, Egbert, and Associates 1987). It is not surprising that the Carnegie Forum on Education and the Economy expressed grave concerns about the fact that after years of surplus teachers, jobs and job seekers in education were roughly in balance in 1985. Until 1995, however, more positions will be available than teachers (Carnegie Forum 1986).

After *A Nation at Risk* called national attention to the "rising tide of mediocrity" in the public schools, a spate of reports dealt with teaching, learning, and educational institutions at all levels. In 1988, the Secretary of Education noted that educational reform is a two-step process and that we now must "exert the will and demonstrate the resolve to overcome the obstacles that block reform" (Bennett 1988, p. 51). Eight points are common to the reports:

1. Progress has been made in improving education, but a second round of reform is needed.
2. Educational policy must improve the conditions for learning and teaching, thus enabling learning to occur.
3. Educational improvement gives cause for optimism because educators realize what needs to be done.
4. Teaching should become more professionalized.
5. Money is important, but so are attitudes, climate, relationships, and community support.
6. Real educational reform will be local in focus because learning is very much an individual act.
7. More collaboration is needed within education as well as beyond to include parents, legislators, governors, and the community.
8. Educators must take new steps to address the special needs of minorities (Green 1987).

Three larger issues, described as "unsettled points," came out of these reports (Green 1987). First, the reports generally call for more confidence in teachers, principals, schools, and school districts, yet they recommend that states be ready to intervene when efforts miss the mark. A primary concern in this area is the matter of decentralizing authority. The reports seem to recognize that education will not be improved "by government decree," but the beliefs about the results are tempered by the fear of what will occur if reforms do not work. A second unsettled issue pertains to "helping versus judging" (p. 12). Authorities outside education are willing to be helpful in improving education, yet at the same time they (especially governors) want to have tangible results as soon as possible in such areas as higher test scores, more peaceful school environments, and more positive attitudes about schools. The issue of assessment remains unsettled, especially regarding who should judge results and how. The third concern deals with leadership versus collaboration. Governors, as noted earlier, need to be involved in educational reform, but ambiguity exists as to exactly how, where, and when they should be involved. Simple calls for leadership and for collaboration without clarifying these issues is unsettling.

Despite desires to the contrary, the teaching profession has continued to remain as a stepchild to other academic fields:

Higher education has exploited teacher education for its own interests, while granting it low status, misplacing it organizationally and programmatically, and seriously underfinancing it. Even the vigorous development effort of the last 10 years has not produced much change; teacher education still sits on the academic street corner, tin cup in hand, begging for the capital to market its product (Howsam 1976, p. 57).

Concerns continue over the status of the teaching profession. Not only has the academic ability of students intending to become teachers declined, as measured by SAT scores from 1973 through 1981: The scores of students planning to major in education have declined more steeply than the scores of other students (Darling-Hammond 1984). The attrition rates of teachers have increased considerably in recent years. The qualifications of newly hired teachers, especially in mathematics and science, indicate that more than half are not certifiable in subjects they are assigned to teach. Beginning salaries for teachers continue to lag behind many other occupations. Perhaps most distressing is the fact that the proportion of teachers who report that they would not enter teaching if they had it to do over again has increased significantly, indicating that their dissatisfaction has increased. The changing role of women in American society continues to have an effect on the status of the teaching profession. The teaching profession can be enhanced because of the women's movement (Sedlak and Schlossman 1986), but an increasing number of women who are qualified to teach are seeking positions outside teaching to make higher salaries.

Interest in educational reform continues unabated (Academy for Educational Development 1985), but it is clear that specific provisions for improving the quality of teachers must involve collaborative efforts between those inside the schools and those external to teaching, including governors. These continuing concerns prompted the Education Commission of the States to identify, as part of its three-year plan for 1987 to 1990, "the momentum of reform" as one of five major forces that will shape educational policy. As top priority issues, the commission focused on change, restructuring schools, and the leadership required for educational progress. State policies need to be created that can empower teachers in decision making, enhance the learning environment for a broader range of students, and improve the curriculum to raise literacy. Restructuring options needs to be considered to facilitate accomplishment of these goals. School funding must be viewed relative to these options for restructuring. School leadership must go beyond a narrow concept of management. A greater number of minorities must enter teaching (Education Commission 1987b).

Collaborative partnerships

One of the issues emerging from educational reform is the desirability of collaborative efforts involving those who are working toward mutually agreeable ends. The Education Commission of the States, in the 1987 meeting of its Steering Committee, observed that both incentives and collaborative partnerships are underused in educational reform. Such incentives and partnerships include state-local collaboration, joint legislative committees, partnerships between schools and colleges to implement reform in the classroom and to improve teacher education, school/college commissions to improve the articulation between high school graduation and college attendance, partnerships designed to build integrated data bases, and interagency task forces that can avoid duplication and reduce waste in providing services.

In particular, collaborative partnerships are needed between public secondary schools and higher education institutions. While these partnerships may focus on teacher training, they can reach beyond to span a broad range of concerns about educating people of all ages (Lederman 1987).

A successful collaborative partnership was the Westchester School Partnership at the State University of New York–Purchase (Gross 1988). The partnership began in 1983 with a five-year funded effort supported by the American Can Company involving 11 school districts and college administrators. The metaphor of a wheel was used to describe the partnership, with colleges at the hub providing a source of continued support, public schools as the spokes, and other organizations, such as businesses or research institutes, as temporary partners. One of the partnership's special features was its major projects in math/science, leadership development, secondary school guidance, economic education, and summer institutes for elementary teachers.

Minorities in Higher Education

The issue of minorities is easy to define, but agreeing on causes and implementing solutions is extremely difficult. The issue is clear: Minorities are insufficiently represented in number and percentage in higher education. "After a short burst of progress in the 1970s, there has been little or no recent progress in entering into programs of higher education that lead to the professional and managerial life of the nation" (Newman 1985a, p. 89). The Commission on Minority Participation in Education and American Life, a joint project of the American Council on Education and the Education Commission of the States, warned that "America is moving backward . . . in efforts to achieve full participation of minority citizens in the life and prosperity of the nation" (Collison 1988, p. 1).

Minorities are underrepresented in higher education, and moreover, their numbers are decreasing, especially blacks. In 1976, blacks represented 9.1 percent of total enrollments in higher education, while Hispanics represented 3 percent. By 1984, these percentages had fallen to 8.7 percent for blacks and had risen to 3.8 percent for Hispanics (U.S. Department of Education 1987, table 131). While the number of Hispanics in higher education is increasing by impressive figures in some areas, they are still underrepresented. Underrepresentation of minorities is especially bad at graduate and professional levels, and the problem is worsening. Blacks earned 820 research doctorates in 1986, 27 percent less than the number earned by blacks in 1976 (Hirschorn 1988). Blacks and Hispanics are less likely than majority students to enter undergraduate programs at universities and four-year liberal arts colleges, undergraduate programs in engineering and the sciences, graduate programs in business, law, medicine, and Ph.D. programs (Newman 1985a).

Ample literature calls attention to the issue of underrepresentation of minorities. In the early 1980s, two reviews of the literature on the subject appeared. *Minority Access to Higher Education* cited the gains made by minorities through the mid-1970s, commenting that parity in access to and choice of college was being approached, if not achieved, because of governmental and institutional support (Preer 1981). Admittedly, problems existed—some colleges had historically low retention rates for minorities, and desegregation efforts in some states threatened historically black colleges. The other review of the literature revealed how the transition from elite to mass higher education in the United States occurred largely because of the presence of federal and state governments (Green 1982). The federal role in education has been limited and specialized in such areas as categorical grants and federal student financial aid, and the state role has been targeted to "brick and mortar issues during the postwar years," yet states were responsible for expanding access and opportunity after World War II (Green 1982, p. 14).

In 1982, the publication of *Minorities in American Higher Education* culminated a two-year project at the Higher Education Research Institute that was aided by a national commission on minorities. Calling attention to the change in mood and direction of the White House in 1980, the book used longitudinal and survey data to analyze the elements associated with the access and attainment of blacks, Chicanos, Puerto Ricans, and American Indians (Astin 1982). It was found that minority students who tended to persist in college were those who performed relatively well in high school, had positive study habits, and had high self-esteem. Living on campus, receiving financial aid, and not having to work were other elements associated with persistence. Having taken a college preparatory curriculum and having high aspirations were significant predictors of satisfaction with college. The commission found that governmental programs played a key role in minorities' access to higher education, and despite the federal government's "overshadowing the primacy of the states' role and responsibility for higher education. . .the states remain the senior partner in higher education" (Astin 1982, p. 128).

Demographic and economic conditions
The pool of traditional college-age students (18- to 24-year-olds) is now contracting and will continue to do so until about 1998, when the influence of the "baby boom echo" will be felt in higher education (State Higher Education Executive Officers 1987a). During the coming years of decline in enrollment of traditional students, minorities will be represented in growing numbers because of higher birth rates and immigration. Minorities currently represent 21 percent of the U.S. population but only 17 percent of the total college enrollment, however. Growth in minorities will be greatest in the South, followed by the Midwest, Northeast, and West. By 1990 in Texas, for example, over 45 percent of the children born will be minority, and 45 years later, fewer than half of Texans will be non-Hispanic whites (p. 7). The transition of America's economy from a manufacturing base to technology and services is under way, and by 2000, 90 percent of the 18 million new jobs will be in service industries (p. 9). Education, including higher education, is expected to be of great importance to job seekers, who will need advanced skills as well as the flexibility to take advantage of retraining and relocation.

The minority gap in access and completion
Just when opportunities exist and minorities are in demand (albeit in some fields more than in others), the gap between what is and what should be for minorities has become prominent (SHEEO 1987b). Minorities are underrepresented in higher education generally—but especially in four-year institutions. Minority enrollment in many (but not all) community colleges approximates their proportional representation in the population. Minorities are more likely to attend public than private institutions. American Indian and Hispanic enrollments are concentrated in two-year institutions, with Hispanics representing 8 percent of the 18- to 24-year-olds but only 5 percent of undergraduates. College enrollment among blacks peaked in 1980 and has declined substantially thereafter. Since 1980, only six states showed increases in college enrollments among blacks at both two-year and four-year institutions. High school graduation rates have increased for minorities in recent years, but the

Current completion rates for whites is 59 percent, compared to 42 percent for blacks, 31 percent for Hispanics, and 39 percent for Native Americans.

proportion of minorities enrolling in college has declined. The decline in the college-going rate is especially evident among young black men: From 1980 to 1984, the number of black men enrolled in higher education dropped 25,000 to 368,000.

The completion rate of minority students is even more alarming. From 1976 to 1984, the number of black college graduates dropped more than 10 percent, from 26,000 to 23,000 (Collison 1987). Current completion rates for whites is 59 percent, compared to 42 percent for blacks, 31 percent for Hispanics, and 39 percent for Native Americans (SHEEO 1987b, p. 18).

Complex causes to a dilemma

The causes for disparities in minority access and achievement are complex and have to do with socioeconomic conditions, psychological and cultural factors, and educational factors. Historically high levels of poverty among minorities, coupled with more recent increases in minority unemployment, have taken heavy tolls in minority communities. In 1982, the median income of blacks and hispanics compared to whites was at the lowest point since 1972. In 1984, three times as many blacks were below the poverty level compared proportionally with whites, with nearly as much reported for Hispanics (SHEEO 1987b, p. 21).

Cultural and psychological factors influence the educational attainment of minorities. Isolation from mainstream role models can be a powerfully negative influence on educational aspirations and attainment. In one study, having attended an integrated high school was positively associated with persistence in college, and having attended a predominately black high school was negatively associated with undergraduate grade point average (Astin 1982). Attitudes found on campuses reflect those of the larger community. Consequently, in the mid-1980s racial incidents in New York City and Philadelphia portended an uncertain future for race relations on many campuses. Recently, a number of protests have occurred on college and university campuses over the low percentage of minorities enrolled as well as declining rates of attendance by minorities.

Educational factors contribute to minorities' access and attainment. If the quality of the student's academic preparation at the time of college entry is the most critical consideration, then a number of secondary school factors are especially important. The strength of the academic program in high school and whether or not the student took college preparatory courses, the level of achievement in high school grades (found to be the single most important predictor of college GPA), aptitude test scores, the student's study habits, and availability of tutoring are contributing factors to reaching college. The educational environment of the college, quality of instruction, financial resources if needed, counseling, and support services all affect minority students' capacities for college-level work.

The common wisdom about reasons for the declining college attendance of blacks is in error (Arbeiter 1987). Incorrect assumptions have to do with changes in the structure of black families, a higher death rate among black teenagers, more black youths in prison, higher drug arrest rates for blacks, and a high birth rate among black women, thus keeping them out of college. The real reasons blacks are not going to college, according to Arbeiter, are that blacks increasingly have chosen to enter the armed services, to work directly in business and industry, or to complete their education in noncollegiate postsecondary schools (1987, p. 16).

The leadership of the states

In reviewing the calls for reform of higher education, state higher education executive officers identified institutional roles and mission, assessment, collaboration between schools and colleges, and minority students' achievements as four of the most critical policy issues. One of the task forces appointed to examine each topic dealt with achievements of minority students. The plan included specific steps (SHEEO 1987c). SHEEOs should establish achievement of minority students as a preeminent concern for higher education. Government must assist in removing economic barriers to college attendance. An institutional planning and reporting process should be put into place to improve minority students' access and achievement. Resources should be found to support minority-related programming. Higher and elementary/secondary education should all be involved when it comes to minority concerns. Institutions should use broader and more effective means of assessing students for admission. Opportunities should be available for minority students at both two-year and four-year schools. Institutional programming should help minority students function more effectively within the institution as well as adapting the institution to the environment. Racial and ethnic diversity should be promoted in professional ranks. Information should be disseminated widely about opportunities in higher education for minority students. The SHEEO plan is especially important because it illustrates the manner in which state leaders have stepped into the gap caused by the lack of leadership at the federal level. State leaders have "the leverage to bring about change, the perspective to ensure that priorities accord with regional conditions, and can encourage the partnerships needed to deal with the issue effectively" (Yavorsky 1988, p. 67).

A 1987 survey of SHEEOs cosponsored by the Education Commission of the States identified six common strategies that state governments have implemented to improve minority participation (Callan 1988). Outreach efforts to schools have used college resources to strengthen the preparation and motivation of low-income and disadvantaged students for college. Graduate and professional schools have increased minority participation rates by targeting selected juniors in high school for later entry to graduate and professional schools. Many states have new services designed to improve the retention of minority students, such as support services, developmental courses, career planning, and psychological counseling. Precollege academic programs strengthen the basic skills and preparation in content of disadvantaged high school students. Financial aid is directed to students based on need and to faculty to increase the number of minority teachers in colleges and universities.

While state leadership is needed to improve both the access and the retention of minorities in higher education, the approach must involve an effort by the entire institution. Fragmented approaches will lead to incomplete solutions; a "seamless fabric of efforts [is needed], extending over the entire institution" (Richardson, quoted in Jaschik 1987g, p. 31). Research completed at the National Center for Postsecondary Governance and Finance focused on 10 majority institutions that achieved success in retaining and graduating minority students (Richardson and Skinner 1988). The research identified profiles of success based on a match between students' characteristics and institutional strategies. One profile included students for whom expectations were high, support was adequate, and self-confidence was evident. Another profile included frequently first-generation college students who had adequate motivation but needed extra support. A third profile was of students who were adequately prepared for college but lacked direction. The final profile was students who persisted "against the odds," often completing their education later as adults. Institutions have an obligation to expand opportunities for minorities, and when minorities succeed, it may be traced to the institution's accepting responsibility and improving its environment through adaptation as well as improving the preparation of students (Richardson and Skinner 1988).

Special effort is needed to increase opportunities for minorities in teaching. In particular, improvement is needed in remuneration, autonomy, and career opportunities at all levels. Such efforts will increase the rewards of teaching, which will make the profession more attractive to minorities (Hatton 1988). While the interest of freshmen in teaching careers has increased markedly—from a low of 4.7 percent in 1982 to 8.1 percent in fall 1987 (Cooperative Institutional Research Program 1987)— the decrease in the percentage of minorities enrolled in colleges and universities is not an optimistic sign.

Program Review in Higher Education
Academic program review is one of the most prominent issues in American higher education (Conrad and Wilson 1985). Program review has been defined as a subset of program evaluation, dealing only with evaluating existing programs, while program evaluation deals with existing and new programs (Conrad and Wilson 1985). Program evaluation, including accreditation, was an activity established in the latter part of the 19th century. It has grown significantly in this century to include voluntary evaluation by regional accrediting associations and by specialized disciplinary and professional organizations, as well as program review by governmental bodies. While academic program review was not used in the early days of state higher education agencies, program review has come into prominence since midcentury as one of four principal functions of statewide boards (along with budgeting, planning, and policy analysis) (Glenny 1985).

Program review can be conceptualized as a part of program evaluation, which is viewed as part of a total system of evaluation of institutions of higher education. A three-part conceptual scheme of institutional evaluation includes state institutional licensing, regional institutional accreditation, and institution-initiated evaluation and planning systems (Kells 1986). States' licensing and review function involves program review in preparation for the initial registration of an academic program with the state, licensure of the professions, and periodic review of academic programs. This procedure is coordinated either by an institution or by a system as part of academic program planning. Accreditation is voluntary and cyclical, usually occurring on a five- or a ten-year basis. Institution-initiated evaluation includes four areas: state or national testing of graduates of professional fields, specialized accreditation of programs, state-mandated program reviews, and institutional reviews of academic programs. The latter two types of evaluation often are coordinated cooperatively by the state, usually through the state higher education agency and the institution. "While state efforts are being enhanced as the external climate becomes more restrictive, the long-term inclination continues to be toward increased formalized, external, nongovernmental, and local institutional efforts and responsibility" (Kells 1986, p. 145). A cautionary note seems in order, however: "Looking to the future, it seems clear that the police powers of government cannot be turned over to voluntary associations" (Harcleroad 1980, p. 6).

The current status of program review

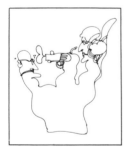

The impetus for academic program review came about as a result of federally initiated review of academic vocational programs in community colleges and a result of the concerns about quality and cost in doctoral programs in universities (Barak 1986). From the 1960s to the 1970s, the purpose of program review shifted from internal assessment by faculty to reviews involving persons external to the campus when decisions about priorities for planning and allocating resources were necessary. Academic program review as currently undertaken has six outstanding characteristics:

1. Program review is widely used, in part because of pressures for accountability and the initiatives of state higher education agencies in reviewing academic programs.
2. Program reviews now are comprehensive, encompassing undergraduate programs and cocurricular areas such as continuing education and student services.
3. The criteria for program review are numerous, complex, and comprehensive, and the process is much more systematic than it once was.
4. The purpose for program review has changed from formative to summative, from generating information to making judgments.
5. Program review now is related more closely to the institutional decision-making process.

6. Attitudes about program review have changed because program review is monitored more closely since it became more important (Barak 1986).

Of interest to this report is the relationship between state and campus in program review. It is a collaborative relationship, especially in the selection of reviewers and the determination of the purpose and scope of the review. In the case of external reviewers and external reviews, institutional officials often consult with staffers from the state higher education agency regarding the identification of reviewers, their credentials and experience, and their suitability for the specific review. As to the approach used in program review, any number of alternative models are available, among them the following four:

1. The goal-based model, where program goals are identified and data are generated to assess the congruence between ends (goals) and means (current program characteristics)
2. The responsive model, which can measure unanticipated consequences and side effects and compare them with program activities.
3. The decision-making model, where information is generated to examine such areas as context, input, process, and product
4. Connoisseurship, where external experts serve as critics for a program (Conrad and Wilson 1985).

The multiple purposes of program review

Program reviews have multiple purposes, perhaps serving to assess a program's productivity, to identify ways to improve quality, to ensure appropriate use of resources, to determine effectiveness, to serve as an aid to planning, or to satisfy requirements of the state higher education agency (Conrad and Wilson 1985). They can be initiated in instances of duplicated programs, questionable quality, a job market with excess demand, high-cost programs, and imbalances between such things as public opinion and perceived need (Melchiori 1982).

A key issue is whether campus and state purposes are compatible—and it is a difficult question that can be answered only when both the state agency and the campus are forthright about the purpose of evaluation and they make a joint decision about which approach to take, which variables to include, and which process to select. For instance, a state agency might believe that program review is necessary to examine low-demand and high-cost programs. The campus may be in the middle of a review for a purpose different from possible program discontinuance. A joint decision between the state agency and the campus is needed to determine whether or not the current institutional evaluation can satisfy the information needs of a process that might end in elimination of the program. Before initiating program review, both campus and state need to agree jointly on the purpose and possible outcome. To do otherwise may invite political intrusion.

The purposes and objectives of program review involve both state and campus interests. In some areas, the state has a predominant interest—perhaps in formulating statewide policies and plans and in identifying possible duplication in programs across different campuses (Wallhaus 1982). On the other hand, campuses have a stake in making decisions about personnel, determining curricula, and defining requirements for admission and graduation. Both the state and the campus have a joint interest in balancing educational and economic interests, and it is in this area where conflict may arise between the state and the campus if, for instance, a campus views a program in educational terms and the state emphasizes its economic aspects.

Both the campus and the state have legitimate interests in collaborative involvement about the purpose and methods of program review. Perhaps the most favorable potential for reducing conflict between the two sides would lie in each campus and state administrative level "sorting out" the focal points of review that can be developed most effectively at a particular level (Floyd 1983, p. 4). Campuses can take the lead, with the state functioning in a supporting role when the purpose of the review is to improve program quality or to develop new alternatives; the state's leadership is needed when the purpose is to deal primarily with issues of planning and resources beyond the boundaries of a single campus. While the Sloan Commission on Government and Higher Education advised states to arrange for periodic reviews of educational program quality at every public college and university using peer review by "highly credible and independent" personnel, it was more uncertain about whether private institutions should be included in the process, envisioning a limited role for the state higher education agency:

Normally the function of the board would be limited to or-

dering the review, publishing the report of the peer group, and in the case of a clearly unfavorable report, recommending appropriate action (Sloan Commission 1980, p. 103).

A more effective relationship should exist between campus and state, with government responsible for planning and supporting the higher education system. The coordinating board should have the responsibility for working closely with the accrediting association "to evaluate the performance of each campus," but the campus's autonomy should be protected:

In academic matters, the integrity of the campus should be fully protected. State officials should not involve themselves directly in the review of academic programs. Rather, they should call upon higher learning institutions periodically to assess such programs and report their findings (Carnegie Foundation 1982, p. 81).

Assessment and Quality: The State's Role
The two terms "assessment" and "quality" reflect much of the momentum in reform of higher education, which began to be affected by the wave of educational reform in elementary and secondary education in the mid-1980s. In many respects, the reform movement was a critique of problems in higher education—emphasis on elective courses rather than attention to the basics, preoccupation with pluralism and diversity, continuing declines in standardized test scores, and a sense that America had lost its competitive edge with other nations. Some asserted that quality was an elusive concept, that it could not be measured, and that it represented different things to different students. Quality, specifically the maintaining of the quality of educational services, was identified as one of two major challenges facing higher education in the 1980s (Floyd 1982). Several principles pertain to quality in higher education:

1. *If comparisons must be made, they should be made between similar types of institutions, at the same level, in the same disciplines, and so forth.*
2. *Quality assessments must identify program goals and objectives and be referenced to them.*
3. *Quality assessments must be based on the variety of attributes.*
4. *The meaning of "quality" is and should be as varied as*

*the purposes behind an assessment, the measurement cri-
teria used, and the group or groups conducting the assessment; herein lie the value and limitations of quality
assessments.*

5. *The teaching-learning function of higher education has
been virtually ignored in quality assessments. Concep-
tually and methodologically, the value-added, input-
environment-output model merits further investigation*
(Lawrence and Green 1980, p. 3).

Early in the reform, those outside the academy, especially
governors and state legislators, realized that states with strong
higher education systems were beginning to move forward with
economic development, job training, high technology, and
more revenue from larger tax bases. The relationship, however,
between external leaders and institutions of higher learning was
confined to selected areas, such as legislative appropriations,
capital requests, and student aid. Governors and legislators
were not as involved in the core academic activities of higher
education. Assessing quality, however, represented one way for
governors and legislators to become more involved. According
to Governor Kean of New Jersey:

*States are interested in higher education for all the same
reasons they consider secondary education important. Governors and legislators are recognizing the fact that a strong
educational presence is of tremendous benefit to a state's
prestige, economy, and quality of life. Then there's the simple fact that states pay for most of higher education. Taxpayers invest very heavily in it, which gives them a strong
interest* (Newman 1985b, p. 13).

The Governors' 1991 Report on Education listed seven task
forces organized around critical issues to be explored from
1986 to 1991 (National Governors' Association 1986). One
task force, chaired by Governor John Ashcroft of Missouri, focused on college quality. In beginning its work, the task force
noted that learning is assumed to take place in college but that
many institutions have no way to demonstrate systematically
that learning has occurred. This task force focused on specific
ways for demonstrating improvement in learning as well as student outcomes and program effectiveness. Six items were formulated in an action agenda: (1) Institutions' roles and mis-

sions should be defined; (2) the fundamental importance of undergraduate education must be emphasized in all institutions; (3) systematic assessment programs using multiple measures should be implemented to assess undergraduates' learning; (4) funding formulas should be adjusted to provide incentives for improving students' learning based on the results of comprehensive assessment programs; (5) a strong commitment to access must be reaffirmed; and (6) accreditation bodies should require campuses to collect and use information about undergraduate student outcomes.

In the "rush to measure," clarity is often a missing element.

Assessment, however, it not a unidimensional activity of administering tests to measure levels of educational achievement. Notions about improving quality have been discussed in higher education, but mandates about assessing students and programs did not begin to appear until after external actors became involved (Marchese 1987). A number of different approaches to assessment have been identified. The assessment center is a process designed to enable observation of desired behaviors. Alverno College pioneered work in "assessment as learning" by developing a curriculum with eight ability levels measured at different performance levels. At the University of Tennessee-Knoxville, assessment consists of monitoring academic programs. Assessment can measure students' learning and growth, as illustrated by the consortium of seven institutions coordinated by Alexander Astin. Assessment can consist of standardized testing. It can be conducted by senior examiners with established reputations as experts in specific fields. In the "rush to measure," clarity about purposes is often a missing element. A campus that responds to state assessment mandates with only a data-gathering effort, "with no eye or connection to improvement, misses the point and sets itself up for a fall" (Marchese 1987, p. 8).

The president of the Educational Testing Service cautioned that an externally imposed mandate on assessment might be a mistake. Institutions must take action; government cannot act for colleges and universities. Higher education needs to be concerned with more than merely minimum competencies. Gaining consensus on fundamental essentials in higher education is difficult because of the diversity of students and institutions. Tests are needed, but they cannot be used alone without human judgment based upon using many sources of information (Anrig 1986).

The role of the states in improving higher education has a

number of facets—improving quality, stimulating assessment, and continuing the reform movement with policy recommendations designed to change higher education in specific ways, such as improving undergraduate education. The five major higher education reports that appeared in 1984 and 1985 emphasized primarily the improvement of undergraduate education (Boyer 1985). In particular, National Institute of Education's (NIEs) report focused on efforts that would set high expectations for students, promote their greater involvement in learning, and implement more effective assessment of students. The Association of American Colleges' (AAC) report focused on redefining the purpose and meaning of the baccalaureate degree. The National Endowment for the Humanities' (NEH) report focused on the humanities and how they could be improved, and Southern Regional Education Board's (SREBs) reports focused on teacher education, remedial programs, and more broadly on undergraduate education.

These higher education reports emerged because of the momentum for reform that grew out of *A Nation at Risk*, focusing on elementary and secondary education, as well as a growing public concern with higher education. While this concern about education spanned both elementary/secondary and postsecondary/higher education, the two sectors are quite different (Ewell 1985b). In higher education, the size of the teaching staff is larger, unlike elementary and secondary education. Students in higher education are not totally lacking in basic skills.

What is different about higher education is that the problems "have largely been those of establishing instructional improvement as a real priority, of changing organizational structures to facilitate improvement and of providing clear incentives for needed change" (Ewell 1985b, p. 5). Given that undergraduate education needs to be improved, the problem becomes one of defining appropriate roles for the state and for each campus. Higher education traditionally is decentralized and self-governing, so authorities resist what is perceived as giving too much authority to agencies outside higher education, including government. State government has a legitimate role in higher education. That role is oriented toward helping define a state purpose for higher education that is at least as great as, if not greater than, the sum of the goals and objectives of each institution, leading to what Ewell conceptualized as two distinct roles for state government:

- State regulatory and funding mechanisms should create an appropriate climate and a set of concrete incentives for inducing institutional self-improvement.
- State government should monitor the performance of the state's higher education system as a whole by collecting appropriate measures of effectiveness at periodic intervals (Ewell 1985b, p. 6).

Higher education has not embraced the reform agenda completely, for a number of reasons. A natural resistance exists to external intrusion into core activities, involving who is to be admitted, what should be taught and by whom, and how academic achievement is to be evaluated and certified. Top administrators in many institutions lack the commitment (Ewell 1985b). Responsibility and accountability for students' success often is fragmented among departments or between academic and student services. Incentives for improvement on campus are insufficient when teaching a large number of students is rewarded more than teaching outcomes in quality and level of performance. It is clear too few mechanisms exist for measuring students' learning and development in higher education.

Despite these problems, a number of institutions have a record of accomplishment in the improvement of undergraduate education (Ewell 1985b). The University of Tennessee–Knoxville, for example, developed a comprehensive instructional evaluation program in response to the Performance Funding Program implemented by the state. Northeast Missouri State University is recognized for measuring students' value-added learning achievement. SUNY–Albany included information on student outcomes in departmental planning and budgeting. Miami-Dade Community College automated teaching and advising with a program of testing for competency and computer support services. St. Petersburg Junior College surveyed outside employers about how well graduates were performing their jobs. Alverno College used a comprehensive assessment program to evaluate students' progress on eight dimensions of learning.

The most successful programs for improving learning have several common characteristics (Ewell 1984, 1985b). First, successful programs focus explicitly on assessment and curricular improvement at the departmental level, not simply at the institutional level. Second, top administrators in successful programs tend to become involved and to support assessment actively. Third, successful programs have explicit, quantitative, and campus-specific data on students' performance.

Assessment in the states is of fairly recent origin. It was not long after the reform movement began to gather momentum in higher education that states actively began pursuing the improvement of undergraduate education. One of the leading organizations working to improve undergraduate education has been the Education Commission of the States. The three-year project on Effective State Action to Improve Undergraduate Education, chaired by Governor Thomas Kean of New Jersey, has been noteworthy in its substantive focus as well as its scope of coverage. Recognizing that undergraduate education must respond to the changing demands of society, a working party defined several specific challenges for consideration and action:

1. to prepare students for a wide range of opportunities beyond college, involving the teaching of basic skills, technical preparation, critical thinking, and interpersonal skills
2. to improve students' preparation for college, with concerns about how and by whom remediation would be done
3. to improve rates of college participation and completion, with specific concerns about retention
4. to meet the educational needs of an increasingly diverse student population, prompting the need to reexamine approaches to teaching and learning in an effort to increase students' involvement
5. to promote students' increased involvement in undergraduate education
6. to assess students' and institutions' performance, recognizing that approaches, instruments, and methods of assessment must be significantly improved
7. to define institutional missions more sharply and communicate them to the public (Education Commission of the States 1986b).

The working party articulated 22 specific recommendations for state leaders, which can be categorized as follows: (1) placing these challenges on the public agenda; (2) incorporating improvement of undergraduate education into comprehensive state strategies, enabling institutions to improve undergraduate education; (3) allocating resources in ways that create a positive environment for change; and (4) encouraging multiple methods of assessment to improve students' and institutions' performance.

As the working party was getting under way, the Education Commission of the States (ECS) surveyed all 50 states to identify initiatives for improving undergraduate education (Boyer and McGuinness 1986). These initiatives can be grouped into five categories: (1) activities targeted to the transition from high school to college, including early assessment as an alternative to placement testing, statements about the skills necessary to succeed in college, identification of standards for exiting high school and entering college, and remedial education; (2) articulation agreements for transfer from two-year to four-year colleges and efforts to identify successful retention programs; (3) broad-based interest in assessment of students' and institutions' performance, with sponsorship by the Ashcroft Task Force under the auspices of the National Governors' Association and efforts by the Education Commission of the States; (4) incentive funding for undergraduate education; and (5) systemwide reviews and comprehensive studies of undergraduate education and higher education in general in a large number of states.

To identify states' actions and activities in assessing students' and institutions' performance, ECS sponsored a survey completed in 1987 (Boyer et al. 1987). It found that only a few states had initiatives for assessment in 1986 but by 1987 two-thirds of the states had initiated such activities. While state leaders have been careful to consider both the design and conduct of assessment as "a matter of institutional prerogative," the states appear to be grouped into three categories of assessment activity. First, about one-third of the state higher education boards viewed their role in assessment as minimal and engaged in coordinating or monitoring activities. Their role, however, was subordinate to institutional initiatives. A common type of activity in this orientation was to collect data on assessment and measure outcomes.

Another group of state higher education boards (about one-half) viewed their role as active, encouraging, promoting, and facilitating institutional initiatives in assessing students and campuses. Some boards required campuses to submit institutional assessment plans; others included assessment in regular state reviews of academic programs, master plans, or campus mission statements. Some boards sponsored statewide assessment conferences; others provided direct financial incentives, such as challenge grants or categorical grants, to support assessment. States in this category appear to be sensitive about their role as mediator among institutions and between campuses and state legislatures.

The third group (about 10 state boards) viewed their role as one in which the state actively designed and implemented assessment programs. Included were states where statewide testing programs were already in place involving selecting assessment instruments and establishing performance criteria. Some states considered assessing system-level outcomes, evaluating the contribution of a state's entire higher education system to the state's economy, goals for literacy, and goals for access.

In 1987, a SHEEO task force on program and institutional assessment formulated a policy statement. The task force conceptualized statewide assessment as "the upper part of a pyramid," with a foundation predicated upon assessment undertaken on each campus and tailored specifically to each institution's circumstances (State Higher Education Executive Officers 1987c). Each degree-granting institution should assess entering students to determine whether they will take courses toward a degree or whether they need remediation before taking courses. All institutions should assess general educational achievement at the undergraduate level. States should develop uniform definitions of graduation, measure retention rates at each campus, and undertake strategies for improving retention, especially for minority students. Students' performance on certification and licensure examinations could be used as a measure of institutional and program quality. Occupational programs should be judged partly by the students' success in finding suitable employment. Community college students' success in transferring to completion programs at four-year institutions should be evaluated. Periodic reports should be compiled of the graduates of each high school in taking basic skills tests, making progress toward degrees, and other similar indicators. Alumni satisfaction should be assessed. States should recognize assessment costs, and states should provide financial incentives for higher- quality instructional programs. Accreditation agencies should use the results of assessment, including assessment of student outcomes, in the accreditation process.

ECS conducted case studies in five states to document state-based approaches to assessment (Boyer and Ewell 1988b). In Colorado, a bill was passed requiring all public colleges and universities to identify objectives for undergraduate education, and campuses were to be held accountable for "demonstrable improvements in student knowledge, capacities, and skills between entrance and graduation" (p. 1). In Missouri, a faculty committee met regularly and formulated recommendations for implementing assessment on each campus. In New Jersey, the College Outcomes Evaluation Program includes a test for sophomores in verbal skills, quantitative reasoning, and critical thinking. New Jersey also used challenge grants as a means to improve institutions' performance in general education and in other areas. In South Dakota, the regents worked with institutions to encourage development of institutional assessment. And in Virginia, a task force worked with the State Council of Higher Education to develop guidelines for assessing students' achievement. The spirit and intent of assessment including state initiatives is reflected in the following statement by the governor of Missouri:

> *Governor Ashcroft issued a challenge to institutional leaders and trustees. . .[that] he would like to see systematic programs of student assessment in place within the next academic year on each campus and that he would recommend for targeted investment funding only those assessment projects that were "practical, doable, and realistic," not those that propose to* study *the assessment issue* (Boyer and Ewell 1988b, p. 4).

In field visits to the five states in 1988, Ewell and Boyer evaluated how state assessment initiatives shaped patterns of institutional response. They investigated the origins of state initiatives, the critical events that shaped the initiatives, and the effects of the initiatives as demonstrated by campuses' responses, discovering differences among the states in three areas: economics (more resources for assessment in Virginia and New Jersey and less in Missouri and South Dakota); political culture (more centralized decision making in Virginia and strong gubernatorial support for assessment in New Jersey and Missouri); and patterns of investment (direct budget allocations per student in Virginia, a flat amount in New Jersey, and selected targeted amounts in the other three states). The states exhibited several thematic modes of implementing assessment. They searched for familiar models to use, often turning to previous experience in elementary and secondary education. The greatest problems with assessment arose from unclear communications between state policy makers and campus leaders, including politicization of the assessment issue. Considerable tension existed over academic and political timetables. For example, conflict and tension can exist between the academic governance calendar and the timetables of politicians concerned about reelection. Significant pressure existed for common standardized achievement testing, although it was recognized that assessment needs to take place at and by individual campuses.

Institutions in the five states were categorized into three patterns of response to assessment. First, some institutions, including major research universities, resisted assessment, and opposition tended to provoke more direct state action to achieve compliance from institutions. The majority of institutions fell into a second category, those that completed only those tasks required by the state. Third, campuses viewed assessment as an opportunity to achieve local initiatives. In such a proactive response, campuses moved ahead of state mandates. While both campus and state leaders need to work cooperatively in meeting timetables and achieving stated goals, this approach appeared to work successfully because it capitalized on institutional initiative and minimized the necessity for the state to take a more aggressive role in implementing the objectives of assessment. Ewell and Boyer, however, did *not* find a correlation between institutional type and assessment initiatives. Both "proactive" and "wait-and-see" institutions represented virtually all types of campuses. While the authors concluded that it was too early to determine the longer-term impact of state mandates for assessment, they observed that assessment is neither a blessing nor a curse. The decision to move ahead with assessment must be debated and resolved on its own merits (Ewell and Boyer 1988).

Summary
The reform movement in higher education followed initial reform efforts in elementary and secondary education after the publication of *A Nation at Risk* in 1983. In higher education, governors and legislators asked fundamental questions about purpose, productivity, and performance. Experts believe that changes in the state structure for higher education will not necessarily lead to improvements in finance, program, or personnel. Organizational structure is a means, not an end in itself,

and the entire process for policy making in higher education needs to be examined.

As a policy issue involving both state government and campuses, minorities in higher education present a vexing problem to campus and state leaders. It is clear that state leadership will be a critical element in implementing solutions to this dilemma, and the current involvement of state higher education executive officers represents a strong beginning toward a solution. While they have state-level dimensions, minority underrepresentation and achievement are problems whose solutions must be implemented by individual campuses.

The states' role in academic program review has been a major concern since the 1970s. While program review initially was faculty initiated on campus, the purpose of program review shifted to more comprehensive, summative judgments about quality, productivity, and effectiveness, and as an aid to planning.

Assessment and quality reflect much of the focus of the higher education reform movement. Assessment is one way to achieve higher quality by evaluating students' learning through outcomes and performance. The momentum to improve quality is not diminishing. On the contrary, more states and more campuses than ever are assessing students' and institutions' outcomes. The more successful programs have active assessment at the departmental level, the involvement of top administrators, and the generation of quantitative and campus-specific data. Assessment is one issue where the involvement of governors has been evident, but their impact remains largely untested. Assessment will continue to present the opportunity for inappropriate intrusion as well as politicization. Governors and other state leaders can serve as the catalysts for identifying assessment as an important activity; however, the process and implementation of assessment must remain within the sphere of colleges and universities.

ANALYSIS AND IMPLICATIONS

The relationship between state governments and higher education can be described as a partnership. Each side is a principal in the joint venture of providing higher and postsecondary education services to students and others. A partnership is not possible under conditions of full accountability or complete autonomy, or when one side defines the relationship unilaterally. Full accountability occurs when higher education functions as a public agency, subject to the controls and regulations pertaining to any other public agency. Complete campus autonomy is achieved when government is uninvolved in campus affairs, other than providing some minimal level of financial support. Theoretically, either policy option is possible, but in operational terms neither option can be considered seriously.

A third option is government's and higher education's coexistence in a partnership. In such an arrangement, the two entities either compete or cooperative. There is no competition between higher education and government, although institutions compete with each other for students, faculty, and research funds. In a partnership, government and higher education have separate goals and operating procedures, yet both sides are necessarily involved in defining their essential relationship. In a real partnership, neither side can define the relationship unilaterally.* Each entity is an organizational hierarchy, and each maintains a "semihierarchical relationship" in relation to the other, characterized by each having partial authority over and partial independence from the other (Zusman 1986).

In many areas, the current partnership between government and higher education is a joint venture where both entities seek ways to work together to achieve mutually desirable ends. Many examples exist of joint and cooperative ventures undertaken by state government and higher education. In economic development in some states, higher education receives subsidies and direct payments for retraining employees and there are incubators for development of small businesses and cooperative programs involving personnel exchanges. Local communities and state governments provide tax breaks to stimulate relocation of business and industry. The presence of higher education facilities in a community help to attract business and industry, not only for continued training and development of workers, but also because of the educational opportunities available and

In a partnership, higher education is less insulated and more involved in public affairs and local communities as well as with state government.

---

*Robert O. Berdahl 1988, personal correspondence.

the "quality of life" that higher education brings to a community.

In a partnership, higher education is less insulated and more involved in public affairs and local communities as well as with state government. Much in this report suggests that higher education has become more involved with the external world. First, state leaders, especially governors, are integrally involved in higher education. Some governors view higher education as a means of revitalizing regional economies, retraining workers and solving problems like the underachievement of minorities and the deterioration of public schools. Second, higher education has greatly increased lobbying at both state and federal levels, propelling higher education into the visible and controversial arena of policy making. Third, higher education has reached out to form collaborative partnerships with external agencies and groups.

The Relationship between State Government And Higher Education

If a partnership accurately describes the relationship between state government and higher education, it is necessary to consider the parameters of this relationship in different areas of policy concern. Two frameworks from the recent literature provide a perspective for analyzing the relationship (see figure 2). In the area of financing public higher education, four models or alternative structures are identified, ranging from a corporate arrangement with maximum institutional flexibility and little direct state control to a state agency approach with a high degree of state control and little institutional flexibility (Curry and Fischer 1986). In the corporate approach, each campus has independent status and freedom of action; the state contracts for services, such as subsidized student "space," research, and public service. Campuses have total control of funds, and state appropriations are made to a third party for payment. The state-aided approach features decentralized control and governance at the campus level, retention of funds raised by the institution, tuition levels set by governing boards, and only state general funds subject to state budgetary control. State involvement increases in the state-controlled approach, with executive and legislative officials involved in decisions like setting salary increases and distributing funds among programs and states having ultimate responsibility for all budgeted funds. Finally, the state agency approach includes little local latitude, with the leg-

FIGURE 2

THE ACCOUNTABILITY/AUTONOMY CONTINUUM

	Minimum State Control and Maximum Campus Autonomy			Maximum State Control and Minimum Campus Autonomy
Models for state financing of public higher education (Curry and Fischer 1986)	Corporate	State aided	State controlled	State agency
State approaches to policy issues (Cross and McCartan 1984)	Laissez-faire	Encouragement	Intervention	Direct support and services

Sources: Curry and Fischer 1986; and Cross and McCartan 1984.

islature having responsibility for funding all operations, funds deposited in the state treasury for disbursement, tuition levels prescribed by the legislature, and preaudit control.

The other framework shown in figure 2 pertains to the state-campus relationship in policy issues, in this instance the provision of adult educational services (Cross and McCartan 1984). The continuum moves from a laissez-faire approach, where states have no role in providing services, to a situation where states provide programs and services. In a laissez-faire environment, states take a hands-off attitude and defer to the campus. When states "encourage," they are involved in planning, setting goals, collecting data, creating incentives, promoting local cooperation, establishing task forces, and sponsoring seminars and conferences. When they "intervene," states resolve issues by delegating responsibility for coordination or centralizing coordination and by regulating providers. Finally, when states provide direct support and services, they actually fund programs and establish statewide programs.

The modal pattern in higher education has been for the state-aided or encouragement approach. The 50 states exhibit significant diversity, however, according to the type of relationship that may have evolved in response to a given policy issue. Indeed, states differ among themselves within the same issue, with some states choosing a more centralized state agency or direct services approach, while other states strongly advocate a decentralized state-aided or even a laissez-faire approach. Varied state approaches to assessment illustrate this diversity. More generally, a fundamental characteristic of American higher education *is* diversity, "an unplanned disorderliness that has permitted different parts to perform different tasks, adapt to different needs, and move in different directions of reform" (Clark 1978, p. 30).

State Leadership in Higher Education

The state higher education agency is in a more visible position than it has been in the past. A majority of the states have had blue ribbon commissions and ad hoc groups studying higher education during the 1980s. In too many cases, however, the focus is on state structure rather than on substantive issues. Some would advocate, however, that one reason for preoccupation with structure is the involvement of governors and legislatures in higher education. The creation of a blue ribbon commission is a logical decision for a governor or legislative leader, and it may alleviate what otherwise would be continued pressure on the governor and legislative leaders for increasing their involvement in higher education. A focus on substance rather than structure, however, will help higher education leaders formulate their own solutions if for no other reason than to prevent solutions from being forced on higher education from without.

Recent years have seen examples of inappropriate actions by trustees and members of governing boards dealing with bureaucratic and political issues. Trustees and governing board members should concentrate on policy making, leaving institutional management to administrators. Trustees and governing board members must be careful about subjecting their institutions to inappropriate political relationships and actions. Violations of this principle are common in the states and appear to be especially evident in community colleges.

Governors' renewed interest in higher education has resulted in increased attention to education in a number of states. In economic development, new partnerships between government and higher education have been forged. A number of states have provided new money for higher education, as evidenced by increased rates of gain in appropriations, thus supporting opportunities for research, training, and public service. In states where these partnerships have been successful—California,

Massachusetts, and Pennsylvania, for example—it is evident that higher education gained financial support because of this involvement. The example from Pennsylvania is instructive:

Proposed legislative efforts would complement an existing model that has had an exciting, innovative, and effective impact on the commonwealth over the last five years. Specifically, I am referring to the Ben Franklin Partnership Program, which is designed to bring together resources of business, educational institutions, and state government to jointly fund projects [that] have as their bottom line the creation of new jobs and retention of existing ones in Pennsylvania. To date, over 19,500 persons have been retrained in technology application, 439 new technology-based companies have been established in our state, 390 companies have expanded, and over 10,600 manufacturing jobs have been created or retained. Pennsylvania has invested over $100 million on these initiatives and I'm happy to report that this share has been matched by a $350 million investment from the private sector, educational institutions, foundations, and other sources. With over 128 different colleges and universities and 2,300 companies from across Pennsylvania participating in this project, the Ben Franklin Partnership Program is the largest, state-sponsored economic development program of its kind in the country (Leventhal 1988).

The difficulties of increased lobbying by higher education are of concern. It appears that higher education has been able to increase its lobbying efforts without moving into the arena of political action committees. As lobbying increases in amount and frequency, the opportunity will continue to exist for inappropriate relationships and intrusion. In some instances, alignments with external groups on certain policy issues will have to be avoided because of the potential for negative impact on higher education.

The benefits to higher education from deregulation and decentralization include strengthening campus management. To facilitate deregulation and increase managerial flexibility on campuses, it is necessary for both higher education and state government to work cooperatively. State actions in this area provide a number of examples. While Volkwein's research (1986a, 1986b, 1987, 1989) has been helpful in examining the relationship between campus quality and regulation, this research needs to be expanded, using a broader base of institutions that includes public colleges as well as research universities and community colleges. It may be in the nonresearch institutions where state funding has been least generous and regulations most excessive.

Financing Higher Education at the State Level
A number of developments bring state support of higher education into sharper focus. In the 1980s, tuition prices rose considerably faster than inflation in both the private and the public sectors. Government and families bore the brunt of cost increases caused by rising tuition, increasing indirect costs, and higher institutional expenditures caused by the provision of more services. State tax appropriations, historically the largest source of revenue in the public sector and a significant source of revenue in the private sector, have been increasingly "flat" during the 1980s and are expected not to increase substantially in the future.

Of special interest are mechanisms for incentive funding, competitive grants, and other innovations to increase the financial support for colleges and universities. These new funding devices serve as the means for infusing new money into higher education. While some might accuse government of implementing funding mechanisms with strings attached, such as requiring colleges to measure outcomes and validate performance criteria, it appears thus far that higher education accepted the challenge and is using the opportunity as the means to improve academic programs, to integrate new knowledge into academic curricula, and to improve educational, support, and student services. Much of the initiative toward reform in response to states' innovations in funding is evidence of the desire to aspire to improved performance and productivity in higher education. Aspiration is one of three ingredients necessary to build a constructive relationship between state government and the university (Newman 1987a). The metaphor applies not only to public universities but also to other colleges and universities. Aspiration includes the commonly shared desire for self-improvement along with the beliefs that effort will lead to improved performance and that a high level of aspiration will act to discourage intrusion.

The other two ingredients for a constructive relationship between state governments and higher education are leadership and tradition. Leadership must come from both higher education and government.

In the best of all worlds, it is a coalition of the board, the governor, the legislative leaders, a community group, the chancellors, the presidents. Because there is such a diversity among states and state universities. . .diverse forces have brought forward the needed aspiration to quality. Part of the difficulty in creating a powerful aspiration for having universities of high quality is that it is tied to the broader issue of the state's self-image (Newman 1987a, p. 91).

Tradition involves the concept of political culture—a shared framework of values along with basic assumptions about political actions used to achieve goals (Elazar 1972; Hanson 1983). The political culture defines the nature of politics and the goals of the political system, and higher education is a fundamental component of the political system. An appropriate role for higher education can be formulated using political subcultures. In a traditionalistic subculture, higher education helps maintain a political and social elite. In a moralistic political culture, higher education is a training ground for those who want to improve government and public services. And in an individualistic political culture, higher education is an instrument for accomplishing ends like economic development, the direction of which is formulated by those who gain control of government in a partisan political environment. Political culture includes the history of how state government interacts with higher education. For example, a tradition of acrimony and distrust, going beyond the partisan machinations inherent in the individualistic political culture, will pose problems for the relationship between government and higher education, while a tradition of mutual respect, high expectations, and constructive relationships will provide a fertile base for increasing productivity.

State-Campus Policy Issues

The four policy issues analyzed in this report present opportunities for intrusion and intervention. Program review, however, illustrates how cooperative endeavors can lead to positive results for both higher education and state government. A similarly productive model might be contemplated involving reform, assessment, and minorities. One must recognize that,

while state-level changes in structure will not necessarily lead to substantive change in higher education, questions about structure and organization are within the legitimate concerns of state leaders. Using blue ribbon commissions as a mechanism to assess current conditions, identify problems, and suggest solutions is within the prerogatives of state leaders. Implementing solutions *cannot* be done by state leaders, however. Higher education must be involved in such commissions, but the academy must *implement* solutions.

As a policy issue, concern about minorities may present higher education with its greatest challenge. The issue involves institutional approaches to both students and faculty and staff: recruiting minorities for admission, improving retention rates for minority students, increasing graduation rates, hiring more minority faculty and staff, and improving the quality of life for minorities on campus. The issue is fundamental because it arises out of the social fabric of our society, and it is linked closely to basic demographic changes now beginning to affect higher education (Hodgkinson 1985). The capacity and the willingness of higher education to respond to this issue will demonstrate the extent to which the academy can deal with a fundamental policy issue of increasing importance, provide educational services to a rapidly growing student cohort, offer education and training that lead to opportunities for employment, improve the tax base of states by raising educational levels and furthering employment goals, and help the states with one of the most serious policy issues of the late 20th century.

Issues pertaining to minorities reflect concerns about access and opportunity, while issues dealing with assessment reflect concerns about educational quality. These issues may create competition or conflict over policy within higher education or between the campus and the state. In a period of ample resources, campus leaders can meet the needs for both access and quality improvement. In a period of scarce resources, however, the perception may exist that campuses are compelled to make hard choices between access and quality, thus creating a dilemma for both campuses and states. Both the campus and the state must work to avoid this dilemma by meeting needs for access as well as improved quality. Indeed, in higher education assumptions have been made about an inherent duality in achieving increased access and improved quality (Madrid 1988; Seneca and Taussig 1987). More recent views posit that the achievement of greater access implies achievement of improved quality. Recent empirical research under way as part of the National Center for Postsecondary Governance and Finance suggests that campuses, by using a process of institutional adaptation through changing the organizational culture, can improve *both* access and quality as well as reduce differences related to race and ethnicity in educational achievement (Skinner and Richardson 1988).

The 1970s witnessed ferment about the proper role of government in program review, and the opportunity was presented for inappropriate governmental intrusion in higher education. Some perceived that program review threatened the accrediting process by undermining the process of peer review. The delicate balance between state agencies and campuses in program review and a movement toward local institutional initiatives in academic program review has been studied. Over time, program review has become aligned more closely with campus decision making, and states have willingly encouraged campuses to initiate program reviews as part of academic planning and decision making. Program review and assessment are related activities, because both have their roots in accountability and campus self-improvement. Program review originated with concerns about high-cost graduate programs and assessment has been concerned with individual learners, but both reflect strong concerns about quality.

Assessment presents a challenge to higher education, because assessment is a mechanism for getting at some of the core policy issues in colleges and universities. Assessment is a vehicle for evaluating student outcomes and institutional performance. Higher education is not accustomed to being scrutinized by the public, but assessment presents the opportunity for validating the benefits ascribed to higher education. Higher education should not be reluctant to have outcomes measured and examined by others. A number of promising approaches to assessment are available. Considerable interest has been shown in assessment by governors and state leaders. Since initial efforts in 1985 and 1986, interest in assessment has increased. Most efforts at assessment involve both states and campuses. Based on the accountability/autonomy continuum presented in figure 2, states' roles in assessment fall generally into the categories of encouragement or intervention. States can encourage assessment by becoming involved in planning and setting goals, by including assessment goals in statewide master plans, by collecting and disseminating data about assessment, by creating incentives involving funding, by promoting campus initiatives and cooperation, by establishing task forces, and by sponsoring conferences. Virtually all of these activities already are under way in selected states.

Assessment and program review are related activities in higher education. Program review, which is related also to accreditation and the broader field of educational evaluation, initially focused on high-cost graduate programs, where assessment tended to be oriented toward questions of efficiency on campus or toward individual learners, especially at the undergraduate level. Educational evaluation has progressed through four generations, including a technical generation, description, the evaluator as judge, and, currently, negotiation, where the evaluator serves as mediator (Lincoln 1988). This fourth generation of evaluation involves a set of constructs about the current status of evaluation. First, the primary foci for evaluation involves stakeholders' claims and issues that emanate from different actors, who themselves have varying claims on both the process and outcome of evaluation. These stakeholders can of course be inside and outside the institution. The second construct applicable to evaluation is that negotiation is the primary role of those who function as evaluators. Evaluators as negotiators must deal with actors and audience who may well have competing or conflicting views about evaluation and its outcomes. Third, in a pluralistic context stakeholders and others have differing or competing ideologies that inform and influence the process of evaluation. Finally, evaluation is "inseparable from its political environment" (p. 12); thus, carrying out evaluation is itself a political event precipitated by those who bargain for their own values and preferences.

Implications for Institutions

While a partnership is an appropriate descriptor of the relationship between state government and higher education, the delineation of roles for government and the academy should not be too precise. The relationship between these two entities is dynamic and reciprocal with somewhat fuzzy boundaries. The dynamic quality of the relationship occurs because the environment for government and higher education is shifting and turbulent. The relationship is reciprocal because each entity depends on the other; higher education, for example, has a vested interest in the health of the state's economy, and the state benefits from the knowledge, technology, and the graduates of colleges and universities. Organizational boundaries, however, must remain somewhat imprecise because of the dynamic and fluid quality of both government and higher education.

The fundamental interests of government and higher education are compatible—and in some instances identical. The state is higher education's "legitimator, benefactor, and protector." Higher education is vital to "the polity, the economy, the culture, in short to the public interest, as transmitter and producer of knowledge, as preparer for work and leisure, as social critic" (Bailey 1975, p. 11). The state has a legitimate interest in higher education, and occasions will arise when that interest will become intrusive. Higher education must protect its own interests. To do so, the academy must be aware of what its interests are in defense of its own institutional autonomy and freedom, beyond some ill-defined notion of minimizing external intrusion into internal institutional affairs. Higher education leaders must define the limits of institutional autonomy and speak out against intrusion of whatever type. "The best protection [of institutional autonomy] is vigilance" (Fisher 1988b, p. 159). Higher education must maintain openness of both its substance and process to respond to the public interest and to preserve autonomy.

The relationship between government and higher education has wide-ranging implications for many leaders and officials in higher education—from system heads to campus presidents and from top administrative staff to college, department, faculty, and student leaders. All of these individuals have a stake in helping define the operational meaning of autonomy for colleges and universities. Autonomy cannot remain an abstract concept; it must be given operational significance by institutional leaders who wish to preserve the freedom of higher education. Institutions will remain free only as long as they act decisively in their own self-interest by identifying the limits of their freedom and the extent to which external interests will be permitted and in what form. At the same time, neither state government nor higher education can be permitted to define the relationship unilaterally. By definition, both sides must be involved in a partnership. Few individuals would disagree that higher education needs the substantive autonomy necessary to protect core academic functions, but many cannot define either the limits or the exact nature of substantive autonomy. This obligation belongs to leadership. It is also difficult to define the nature and limits of procedural autonomy, and it is in the area of procedural autonomy where the greatest number of intrusions have occurred and where the greatest threat to institutional freedom exists. Actions taken to increase managerial flexibility and the decision-making authority of institutional officials have restored balance to the relationship between government and higher education. These relations were becoming increasingly skewed toward public authority in the name of accountability and away from campus prerogatives. Higher education must continue to make its own case in the forum of public policy, because it is in this forum where legislative decisions can be made to help restore and maintain the autonomy that is so necessary.

Implications for Research and Policy Making
Numerous implications for scholarly research grow out of this monograph. A number of policy issues that were analyzed in this report are new to the topic of the states and higher education, and the literature is only beginning to explore the facets of these issues. Much more needs to be learned about the issues themselves as well as their implications for institutional practice, research, and scholarship. These issues include economic development, incentive funding, tuition prepayment and savings plans, assessment of student and institutional outcomes, and the reform movement and its implications for undergraduate education.

Not only does the need exist to generate information about these policy issues to provide detail about their major characteristics and features; the need also exists for different types of research on the policy issues. First, descriptive research is needed to generate more information about the issues. We need a better understanding of the roles of key state governmental offices and actors whose decisions affect higher education—governors and their staffs, legislators and legislative staffs, especially leadership, program, and fiscal committees, the state higher education agency and its component parts and other agencies that deal with higher education, the central offices of consolidated and multicampus systems, and individual campuses. These roles vary, sometimes significantly, across policy issues and through time. During times of serious constraints on resources, for instance, private institutions in those states with sizable private sectors likely will be interested in program review in areas served by both private and public institutions.

Beyond the need for information, the need for analyses of

salient policy issues in higher education is growing. These analyses need to examine policy issues across states and to investigate multiple issues within states. To what extent, for instance, do the same policy issues have similar impact across different states? If differences exist, what begins to account for them? How are different policies treated in the same state by different sectors, institutions, and constituent groups? What do these differences indicate about higher education and about state government? The comparative dimension takes into account how an issue differs across states and how issues differ within states. The need for research calls for quantitative research methods like multivariate statistical analyses used in the identification of the environmental determinants of policy. The need also is apparent for qualitative research, including field observation and interviews with key actors and relevant others. Grounded theory and naturalistic approaches could be useful in generating propositions and hypotheses about policy making and state-campus relationships in formulating and implementing policy. Longitudinal studies, while difficult to complete, are especially compelling, as they can provide contextually rich explanations for the development, for instance, of a state's external political traditions over time as these traditions relate to the development of a state higher education system (Fisher 1988a).

This report contains implications for those who formulate policy. It must be recognized that higher education, especially in the policy issues analyzed in this report, is an integral part of the political process. If higher education leaders and policy makers do not have identical interests, their interests are clearly related and at times mutually reinforcing. It is in their own best interests to work together to resolve problems and translate issues into policy decisions. Policy makers would do well to balance public perceptions with the particular situation in that policy domain on campus before formulating proposals for legislative action. Inappropriate action as a result of a perception about the need to contain costs, for instance, may have longer-term negative effects if appropriations are reduced, funds for new programs are eliminated, or unreasonable regulations are levied in the name of efficiency. A true partnership between state government and higher education will have unmistakable features—ample communication between governmental staff and higher education leaders, higher education leaders' clear and accurate articulation about their needs and problems, a visible presence of policy makers on campus and higher education leaders in the legislature, and approaches to lobbying characterized by honesty, accuracy, and a willingness to cooperate and compromise with the other side.

REFERENCES

The Educational Resources Information Center (ERIC) Clearinghouse
on Higher Education abstracts and indexes the current literature on
higher education for inclusion in ERIC's data base and announcement
in ERIC's monthly bibliographic journal, *Resources in Education*
(RIE). Most of these publications are available through the ERIC
Document Reproduction Service (EDRS). For publications cited in this
bibliography that are available from EDRS, ordering number and price
are included. Readers who wish to order a publication should write to
the ERIC Document Reproduction Service, 3900 Wheeler Avenue,
Alexandria, Virginia 22304. (Phone orders with VISA or MasterCard
are taken at 800/227-ERIC or 703/823-0500). When ordering, please
specify the document (ED, HE, or UD) number. Documents are
available as noted in microfiche (MF) and paper copy (PC). Because
prices are subject to change, it is advisable to check the latest issue of
Resources in Education for current cost based on the number of pages
in the publication.

Academy for Educational Development. 1985. *Teacher Development
in Schools: A Report to the Ford Foundation*. New York: Author.

Adler, Madeleine Wing, and Frederick S. Lane. 1985. "Governors
and Higher Education: Politics, Budgeting and Policy Leadership."
State Government 58(2): 68–73.

AGB Reports. 1984. "Minority Trustees Face Special Challenges"
26(5): 20–25.

Altbach, Philip G. 1980. *University Reform: An International
Perspective*. AAHE-ERIC Higher Education Report No. 10.
Washington, D.C.: American Association for Higher Education. ED
202 448. 61 pp. MF–$1.07; PC–$7.73.

American Association of State Colleges and Universities. 1986a. *The
Higher Education–Economic Development Connection: Emerging
Roles for Public Colleges and Universities in a Changing Economy*.
Washington, D.C.: Author.

————. 1986b. *Issues in Higher Education and Economic
Development*. Washington, D.C.: Author.

————. 1987. *Exploring Common Ground: A Report on Business/
Academic Partnerships*. Washington, D.C.: Author.

————. 7 November 1988. "Tuition Prepayment vs. Tuition
Savings." *Memo to the President* 28(18): 3.

Anderson, Richard E. 1988. "College Savings and Prepayment
Plans." *Capital Ideas* 2(3–4): 1–15.

Angel, Dan. 1980. "How to Play the State Capitol Game." *AGB
Reports* 22(5): 41–44.

Anrig, Gregory R. 1986. "A Message for Governors and State
Legislators: The Minimum Competency Approach Can Be Bad for
the Health of Higher Education." Washington, D.C.: American

Association for Higher Education. ED 281 404. 9 pp. MF–$1.07; PC–$3.85.

Arbeiter, Solomon. 1987. "Black Enrollments: The Case of the Missing Students." *Change* 19(3): 14 + .

Arns, Robert G., and William Poland. 1980. "Changing the University through Program Review." *Journal of Higher Education* 51(3): 268–84.

Astin, Alexander W. 1982. *Minorities in American Higher Education*. San Francisco: Jossey-Bass.

Astin, Alexander W., and Frank Ayala. 1987. "A Consortial Approach to Assessment." *Educational Record* 68(3): 47–51.

Atiyeh, Victor G. 1986. "Why I Took Grown-ups Back to School." *Currents* 12(2): 34.

Atwell, Robert H. 1987. "The Patchwork Unravels: Why Student Aid Is Not Delivering." *Educational Record* 68(3): 7–11.

Atwell, Robert H., and Arthur M. Hauptman. 1986. "The Politics of Tuition." *Educational Record* 67(2–3): 5–6.

Bailey, Stephen K. 1975. "Education and the State." In *Education and the State*, edited by John F. Hughes. Washington, D.C.: American Council on Education.

Barak, Robert J. 1982. *Program Review in Higher Education: Within and Without*. Boulder, Colo.: National Center for Higher Education Management Systems. ED 246 829. 137 pp. MF–$1.07; PC–$14.01.

———. 1986. "A Perspective on the Antecedents, Present Status, and Future Developments of Academic Program Review in Higher Education." Paper presented at the annual meeting of the Association for the Study of Higher Education, February, San Antonio, Texas. ED 268 887. 34 pp. MF–$1.07; PC–$5.79.

Beachler, Judith Anne. 1985. "Higher Education and Economic Development: A Relationship." Paper prepared for the Pennsylvania House Subcommittee on Higher Education, March, Harrisburg. ED 255 152. 31 pp. MF–$1.07; PC–$5.79.

Bennett, William J. 1988. *American Education: Making It Work*. Washington, D.C.: U.S. Government Printing Office.

Berdahl, Robert O. 1971. *Statewide Coordination of Higher Education*. Washington, D.C.: American Council on Education.

———. 1977. "Legislative Program Evaluation." In *Increasing the Public Accountability of Higher Education*, edited by John K. Folger. New Directions for Institutional Research No. 16. San Francisco: Jossey-Bass.

———. 1980. "Coordinating and Governing Boards: Complementary or Conflicting Roles." *Vestes* 23(2): 9–18.

Bernstein, Alison. 1985. "Government by Confrontation." *Change* 17(2): 8–9.

Bernstein, Melvin H. 1985. "Forging New Legislative Alliances: Higher Education in the State Capital." *Educational Record* 66(3): 30–31.

Beyle, Thad L. 1983. "Governors." In *Politics in the American States: A Comparative Analysis*, edited by Virginia Gray, Herbert Jacob, and Kenneth N. Vines. 4th ed. Boston: Scott, Foresman & Co.

Bloland, Harland G. 1985. *Associations in Action: The Washington, D.C. Higher Education Community.* ASHE-ERIC Higher Education Report No. 2. Washington, D.C.: Association for the Study of Higher Education. ED 261 642. 135 pp. MF–$1.07; PC–$14.01.

Blumenstyk, Goldie. 6 July 1988. "Questions Raised about Board's Independence as Oregon's Search for College Chief Stalls." *Chronicle of Higher Education* 34: 14–15.

Bok, Derek. 1982. *Beyond the Ivory Tower: Social Responsibilities of the Modern University.* Cambridge, Mass.: Harvard Univ. Press.

Boyer, Carol M. 1985. *Five Reports: Summary of the Recommendations of Recent Commission Reports on Improving Undergraduate Education.* Report No. PS-85-3. Denver: Education Commission of the States.

Boyer, Carol M., and Peter T. Ewell. 1988a. "State-Based Approaches to Assessment in Undergraduate Education." Report No. PS-88-2. Denver: Education Commission of the States.

———. 1988b. "State-Based Case Studies of Assessment Initiatives in Undergraduate Education." Report PS-88-3. Denver: Education Commission of the States.

Boyer, Carol M., Peter T. Ewell, Joni E. Finney, and James R. Mingle. 1987. "Assessment and Outcomes Measurement: A View from the States." *AAHE Bulletin* 39(7): 8–12. ED 284 482. 63 pp. MF–$1.07; PC–$7.73.

Boyer, Carol M., and Aims C. McGuinness, Jr. 1986. "State Initiatives to Improve Undergraduate Education: ECS Survey Highlights." *AAHE Bulletin* 38(6): 3–7. ED 265 800. 6 pp. MF–$1.07; PC–$3.85.

Boyer, Ernest L. 1982. "Control of the Campus: Essay on Governance." *AGB Reports* 24(6): 4–10.

Brademas, John. 1987. *The Politics of Education: Conflict and Consensus on Capitol Hill.* Norman: Univ. of Oklahoma Press.

Breneman, David C., and Chester E. Finn, Jr. 1978. *Public Policy and Private Higher Education.* Washington, D.C.: The Brookings Institution.

Breunig, Robert H. 1980. "Lessons from Proposition 9." *CASE Currents* 6(9): 22–26.

Brimelow, Peter. 30 November 1987. "The Untouchables." *Forbes* 140(12): 140–50.

California Postsecondary Education Commission. 1987. *Funding Excellence in California Higher Education*. Report No. 87-18. Sacramento: Author.

Callan, Patrick M. 1982. "State-Level Governance Issues." Unpublished paper. Denver: Education Commission of the States.

———. 1984. "Lessons from Colorado." In "State Deregulation and Management Flexibility." *AAHE Bulletin* 36(10): 3–8.

———. 1988. "Minority Degree Achievement and the State Policy Environment." *Review of Higher Education* 11(4): 355–64.

Carnegie Council on Policy Studies in Higher Education. 1976. *The States and Private Higher Education*. San Francisco: Jossey-Bass.

Carnegie Forum on Education and the Economy. 1986. *A Nation Prepared: Teachers for the 21st Century*. New York: Author. ED 268 120. 168 pp. MF–$1.07; PC not available EDRS.

Carnegie Foundation for the Advancement of Teaching. 1982. *The Control of the Campus*. Washington, D.C.: Author.

Caruthers, J. Kent, and Joseph L. Marks. 1988. *State Funding of Higher Education for Quality Improvement in the SREB States*. Atlanta: Southern Regional Education Board.

Clark, Burton R. 1978. "The Insulated Americans: Five Lessons from Abroad." *Change* 10(10): 24–30.

Clarke, Lynn B. 1981. "A Tale of Tallahassee: Lobbying the State Legislature." *CASE Currents* 7(1): 8–11.

Cole, Richard T. 1988. "Taking Stock: A Review of the Impact of the Governor's Commission on the Future of Higher Education." Lansing, Mich.: Governor's Commission.

College Entrance Examination Board. 1987. *Trends in Student Aid: 1980 to 1987*. Washington, D.C.: Author. ED 288 486. 15 pp. MF–$1.07; PC not available EDRS.

———. 1988. *Invitational Conference on College Prepayment and Savings Plans*. New York: Author.

Collison, Michele. 9 December 1987. "More Young Black Men Choosing Not to Go to College." *Chronicle of Higher Education* 34: 1+.

———. 25 May 1988. "Neglect of Minorities Seen Jeopardizing Future Prosperity." *Chronicle of Higher Education* 34: 1+.

Commission on the Future of Higher Education. 1984. "Putting Our Minds Together: New Directions for Michigan Higher Education." Final Report of the Governor's Commission on the Future of Higher Education in Michigan. Lansing, Mich.: Author.

Commission on Minority Participation in Education and American Life. 1988. "One-Third of a Nation." Report prepared for the American Council on Education and Education Commission of the States. Washington, D.C.: Author.

Conrad, Clifton F., and Richard F. Wilson. 1985. *Academic Program*

Reviews: Institutional Approaches, Expectations, and Controversies.
ASHE-ERIC Higher Education Report No. 5. Washington, D.C.:
Association for the Study of Higher Education. ED 264 806. 111
pp. MF–$1.07; PC–$12.07.

Cooperative Institutional Research Program. 1987. "Interest in
Teaching Careers Rising: Technology and Nursing Careers Falling
Sharply." Freshman Survey Report. Los Angeles: UCLA, Higher
Education Research Institute.

Cordes, Colleen. 28 January 1987. "Quest to Make U.S. More
Competitive Could Be a Boon to Higher Education." *Chronicle of
Higher Education* 33: 1+ .

Coughlin, Cletus C., and O. Homer Erekson. 1986. "Determinants of
State Aid and Voluntary Support of Higher Education." *Economics
of Education Review* 5(2): 179–90.

Creswell, John W., Ronald W. Roskens, and Thomas C. Henry.
1985. "A Typology of Multicampus Systems." *Journal of Higher
Education* 56(1): 25–37.

Cross, K. Patricia, and Anne-Marie McCartan. 1984. *Adult Learning:
State Policies and Institutional Practices*. ASHE-ERIC Higher
Education Report No. 1. Washington, D.C.: Association for the
Study of Higher Education. ED 246 831. 162 pp. MF–$1.07; PC–
$16.36.

Curry, Denis J., and Norman M. Fischer. 1986. "Public Higher
Education and the State: Models for Financing, Budgeting, and
Accountability." Paper presented at the annual meeting of the
Association for the Study of Higher Education, February, San
Antonio, Texas. ED 268 886. 36 pp. MF–$1.07; PC–$5.79.

Darling-Hammond, Linda. 1984. *Beyond the Commission Reports:
The Coming Crisis in Teaching*. Report R-3177-RC. Santa Monica,
Cal.: Rand Corporation.

Davis, William E. 1988. "Presidential Perspectives." *The Green
Sheet* 4/88. Washington, D.C.: NASULGC.

DiBiasio, Daniel A. 1986. "Higher Education under Study: A
Comparative Analysis of Six Statewide Reports." Paper presented
at the annual meeting of the Association for the Study of Higher
Education, February, San Antonio, Texas. ED 268 894. 42 pp.
MF–$1.07; PC–$5.79.

Doyle, Denis P., and Terry W. Hartle. 1986. "Student-Aid Muddle."
Atlantic Monthly 257(2): 30–34.

Doyle, Peter H., and Candice Brisson. 1985. *Partners in Growth:
Business–Higher Education Development Strategies*. Washington,
D.C.: Northeast-Midwest Institute, Center for Regional Policy.

Dressel, Paul, ed. 1980. *The Autonomy of Public Colleges*. New
Directions for Institutional Research No. 26. San Francisco: Jossey-
Bass.

Dreyfus, Lee Sherman. 1982. "An Educational Agenda with a Public Mission." *Journal of General Education* 34(2): 135–42.

Education Commission of the States. 1986a. "Living on the Leading Edge: State Policy Issues for Education and Economic Development in a Global Economy." ECS Working Paper PS-86-2. Denver: Author.

―――. 1986b. *Transforming the State Role in Undergraduate Education.* Report of the Working Party on Effective State Action to Improve Undergraduate Education. Report No. PS-86-3. Denver: Author. ED 275 219. 45 pp. MF–$1.07; PC–$5.79.

―――. 1987a. "Assessment and Outcomes Measurement—A View from the States." Report of the Working Party on Effective State Action to Improve Undergraduate Education. Report No. PS-87-1. Denver: Author. ED 282 482. 63 pp. MF–$1.07; PC–$7.73.

―――. 1987b. "Collaboration: Teamwork to Get Things Done." Paper prepared by the ECS Steering Committee. Denver: Author.

―――. 1987c. *The Evolving Reform Agenda.* Denver: Author.

Elazar, Daniel J. 1972. *American Federalism: A View from the States.* 2d ed. New York: Thomas Y. Crowell.

Enarson, Harold H. 1980. "Quality and Accountability: Are We Destroying What We Want to Preserve?" *Change* 12(7): 7–10.

Engel, Robert E., and Paul P.W. Achola. 1983. "Boards of Trustees and Academic Decision Making: A Review of Literature and Research." *Review of Educational Research* 53(1): 55–74.

Evangelauf, Jean. 2 December 1987. "Student Financial Aid Reaches $20.5 Billion but Fails to Keep Pace with Rising College Costs, Study Finds." *Chronicle of Higher Education* 34: 33 + .

Ewell, Peter. 1984. *The Self-Regarding Institution: Information for Excellence.* Boulder, Colo.: National Center for Higher Education Management Systems. ED 256 266. 110 pp. MF–$1.07; PC–$12.07.

―――. 1985a. *Assessing Educational Outcomes.* New Directions for Institutional Research No. 47. San Francisco: Jossey-Bass.

―――. 1985b. *Levers for Change: The Role of State Government in Improving the Quality of Postsecondary Education.* Denver: Education Commission of the States. ED 282 509. 39 pp. MF–$1.07; PC–$5.79.

―――. 1987. "Assessment: Where Are We?" *Change* 19(1): 23–28.

Ewell, Peter T., and Carol M. Boyer. 1988. "Acting Out State-Mandated Assessment: Evidence from Five States" *Change* 20(4): 40–47.

Feasley, Charles E. 1980. *Program Evaluation.* AAHE-ERIC Higher Education Report No. 2. Washington, D.C.: American Association for Higher Education. ED 187 269. 68 pp. MF–$1.07; PC–$7.73.

Finn, Chester E., Jr. 1984a. "The Roots of Reform." *Social Policy* 15(2): 16–17.

————. 1984b. "Trying Higher Education: An Eight-Count Indictment." *Change* 16(4): 28–33 + .

Fishbein, Estelle A. 1978. "The Academic Industry—A Dangerous Premise." In *Government Regulation of Higher Education*, edited by Walter C. Hobbs. Cambridge, Mass.: Ballinger.

Fisher, Lois. 1988a. "The External Political Traditions: Their Development and Continuing Impact on the Nation of Two Public Systems of Higher Education." Paper presented at the annual meeting of the Association for the Study of Higher Education, November, St. Louis, Missouri.

————. 1988b. "State Legislatures and the Autonomy of Colleges and Universities: A Comparative Study of Legislatures in Four States, 1900–1979." *Journal of Higher Education* 59(2): 133–62.

Fleming, Robben W. 1978. "Who Will Be Regulated, and Why?" In *Government Regulations of Higher Education*, edited by Walter C. Hobbs. Cambridge, Mass.: Ballinger.

Floyd, Carol Everly. 1982. *State Planning, Budgeting, and Accountability*. AAHE-ERIC Higher Education Report No. 6. Washington, D.C.: American Association for Higher Education. ED 224 452. 58 pp. MF–$1.07; PC–$7.73.

————. 1983. "Balancing State and Institutional Perspectives in the Implementation of Effective State-Level Academic Program Review." Paper presented at the annual meeting of the Association for the Study of Higher Education, March, Washington, D.C. ED 232 551. 21 pp. MF–$.107; PC–$3.85.

Folger, John. 1977. "Prospects for Higher Education Finance in the Next Decade." *Journal of Education Finance* 3(2): 187–88.

————. 1983. "Financing Quality in a Period of Austerity." In *Survival in the 1980s: Quality, Mission, and Financing Options*, edited by Robert A. Wilson. Tucson: Univ. of Arizona, Center for the Study of Higher Education.

Folger, John, and Robert O. Berdahl. 1988. "Patterns in Evaluating State Higher Education Systems: Making a Virtue out of Necessity." Document No. RR 87:3. College Park, Md.: National Center for Postsecondary Governance and Finance.

Folger, John K., and Aims C. McGuinness, Jr. 1984. *Catalog of Changes*. Denver: Education Commission of the States. ED 255 164. 73 pp. MF–$1.07; PC–$7.73.

Ford, William D. 1980. "Send Us a Message!" *AGB Reports* 22(4): 16–18.

Fox, Edward A. 1987. "The Patchwork Is Secure: Student Aid Delivers with Flexibility." *Educational Record* 68(3): 13–16.

Frances, Carol. 1985. "Why Tuition Keeps Going Up." *AGB Reports* 27(2): 24–31.

Gardner, John W., Robert H. Atwell, and Robert O. Berdahl. 1985. *Cooperation and Conflict: The Public and Private Sectors in Higher Education*. Washington, D.C.: Association of Governing Boards of Universities and Colleges. ED 263 815. 71 pp. MF–$1.07; PC–$7.73.

Gilley, J. Wade, and Kenneth A. Fulmer. 1986. "A Question of Leadership, or To Whom Are the Governors Listening?" Paper prepared for the Center for Policy Studies in Education, George Mason University, Fairfax, Virginia. ED 282 489. 9 pp. MF–$1.07; PC–$3.85.

Gilley, J. Wade, Kenneth A. Fulmer, and Sally J. Reithlingshoefer. 1986. *Searching for Academic Excellence*. New York: American Council on Education/MacMillan Publishing Co.

Glenny, Lyman A. 1985. *State Coordination of Higher Education: The Modern Concept*. Denver: State Higher Education Executive Officers. ED 270 070. 27 pp. MF–$1.07; PC–$5.79.

Glenny, Lyman A., and Frank M. Bowen. 1977. "State Intervention in Higher Education." A report prepared for the Sloan Commission on Government and Higher Education, Cambridge, Massachusetts. ED 184 427. 103 pp. MF–$1.07; PC–$12.07.

Gove, Samuel K. 1985. "Election of the Board of Trustees of the University of Illinois." Paper presented at the annual meeting of the American Political Science Association, August, New Orleans, Louisiana.

———. 1986. "Politics and the Elected Board." *AGB Reports* 28(5): 33–35.

Gove, Samuel K., and John Carpenter. 1977. "State Lobbying for Higher Education." *Educational Record* 58(4): 357–72.

Governor's Commission on Excellence in Higher Education (Alan P. Hoblitzell, chair). 1986. "Higher Education: An Investment in Excellence." Paper prepared for Governor Harry Hughes, Annapolis, Maryland.

Graham, Hugh D. 1987. "Structure and Governance in Higher Education: Maryland and the Nation." Paper prepared for the Maryland Institute for Policy Analysis and Research, Univ. of Maryland.

Green, Joslyn. 1987. *The Next Wave: A Synopsis of Recent Education Reform Reports*. Report TR-87-1. Denver: Education Commission of the States.

Green, Kenneth C. 1981. "Program Review and the State Responsibility for Higher Education." *Journal of Higher Education* 52(1): 67–80.

———. 1982. *Government Support for Minority Participation in Higher Education*. AAHE-ERIC Higher Education Report No. 9. Washington, D.C.: American Association for Higher Education. ED 226 688. 65 pp. MF–$1.07; PC–$7.73.

Gregory, Dennis E. 1984. "Financial Assistance by States to Independent Institutions of Higher Education." *Journal of Education Finance* 10(1): 50–63.

Gross, Theodore L. 1988. *Partners in Education: How Colleges Can Work with Schools to Improve Teaching and Learning.* San Francisco: Jossey-Bass.

Gupta, Himanee. 1985. "Corridors of Power." *Currents* 11(1): 9–13.

Hanson, Russell L. 1983. "The Intergovernmental Setting of State Politics." In *Politics in the American States: A Comparative Analysis,* edited by Virginia Gray, Herbert Jacob, and Kenneth N. Vines. 4th ed. Boston: Scott, Foresman & Co.

Harcleroad, Fred F. 1980. *Accreditation: History, Process, and Problems.* AAHE-ERIC Higher Education Report No. 6. Washington, D.C.: American Association for Higher Education. ED 198 774. 60 pp. MF–$1.07; PC–$7.73.

Harcleroad, Fred F., and Allan W. Ostar. 1987. *Colleges and Universities for Change.* Washington, D.C.: AASCU Press.

Hardesty, Robert I. 12 October 1988. "When Politics Intrudes into a University, It Threatens to Poison Higher Education." *Chronicle of Higher Education* 35: 1–2.

Hartmark, Leif S., and Edward R. Hines. 1986. "Politics and Policy in Higher Education: Reflections on the Status of the Field." In *Policy Controversies in Higher Education,* edited by Samuel K. Gove and Thomas M. Stauffer. Westport, Conn.: Greenwood Press.

Hatton, Barbara R. 1988. "A Game Plan for Ending the Minority Teacher Shortage." *NEA Today* 6(6): 66–69.

Healy, Timothy S. 1984. "A Delicate Balance: The Need for Unity in Public and Private Education." *Currents* 10(7): 8–12.

Heftel, Cec. 1984. "Out of the Ivory Tower and into the Lobby." *AGB Reports* 26(1): 11–13.

Henderson, Cathy. 1987. "How Indebted Are Four-Year College Graduates?" *Educational Record* 68(3): 24–29.

Herzik, Eric B. 1985. "The Governors' State-of-the-State Addresses: A Focus on Higher Education." *State Government* 58(2): 65–66.

Hines, Edward R. 1987. "Multicampus Universities and Consolidated Systems." *Grapevine* No. 336. Normal: Illinois State Univ., Center for Higher Education.

———. 1988a. *Appropriations of State Tax Funds for Operating Expenses of Higher Education.* Washington, D.C.: National Association of State University and Land-Grant Colleges.

———. 1988b. "State Support of Higher Education: A 20-Year Contextual Analysis Using Two-Year Percentage Gains in State Tax Appropriations." Paper presented at the annual conference of the National Center for the Study of Collective Bargaining, Baruch College, April, New York, New York.

Hines, Edward R., and Leif S. Hartmark. 1980. *Politics of Higher Education*. AAHE-ERIC Higher Education Report No. 7. Washington, D.C.: American Association for Higher Education. ED 201 263. 85 pp. MF–$1.07; PC–$10.13.

Hirschorn, Michael W. 3 February 1988. "Doctorates Earned by Blacks Decline 26.5 Percent in Decade." *Chronicle of Higher Education* 34: 1 + .

Hobbs, Walter C., ed. 1978. *Government Regulation of Higher Education*. Cambridge, Mass.: Ballinger.

Hodgkinson, Harold L. 1985. *All One System: Demographics of Education, Kindergarten through Graduate School*. Washington, D.C.: Institute for Educational Leadership. ED 261 101. 22 pp. MF–$1.07; PC not available EDRS.

Holmes, Robert A. 1983. "How to Work with Your State Legislatures." *AGB Reports* 25(4): 24–27.

Howsam, Robert B., ed. 1976. *Educating a Profession*. Washington, D.C.: AACTE, Bicentennial Commission of Education for the Profession of Teaching. ED 117 053. 180 pp. MF–$1.07; PC–$18.30.

Hoy, John D., and Melvin H. Bernstein. 1981. *Business and Academia: Partners in New England's Economic Renewal*. Hanover, N.H.: Univ. Press of New England.

Hyatt, James A., and Aurora A. Santiago. 1984. *Incentives and Disincentives for Effective Management*. Washington, D.C.: National Association of College and University Business Officers. ED 257 347. 66 pp. MF–$1.07; PC–$7.73.

Independent Commission on the Future of the State University. 1985. *The Challenge and the Choice*. Albany: State Univ. of New York.

Jaschik, Scott. 2 April 1986a. "Community Colleges Are Changing Their Roles to Meet Demands for New Types of Job Training." *Chronicle of Higher Education* 32: 13 + .

———. 16 April 1986b. "States' Plans Link Small Businesses and Universities." *Chronicle of Higher Education* 32: 1 + .

———. 29 January 1986c. "University-Industry-Government Projects: Promising Too Much Too Soon?" *Chronicle of Higher Education* 32: 1 + .

———. 11 March 1987a. "Charges of Impropriety Bring Calls for Closer Scrutiny of Oklahoma Colleges." *Chronicle of Higher Education* 33: 25 + .

———. 18 November 1987b. "Chief of Wisconsin University System Ignites Passions with Proposals to Waive Tuition for Minority Students." *Chronicle of Higher Education* 34: 24–25.

———. 30 September 1987c. "College Store Group Pressured to Halt 'Wildcat' Lobbying." *Chronicle of Higher Education* 34: 18 + .

———. 18 November 1987d. "Governors and Legislators Press State Boards to Exert More Leadership over Public Colleges." *Chronicle of Higher Education* 34: 25 + .

———. 9 September 1987e. "Intense Lobbying by Texas Colleges Wins Increases for Many, but Two-Year Institutions Are Left Out." *Chronicle of Higher Education* 34: 22 + .

———. 23 September 1987f. "Louisiana's Public Colleges, Racked by Budget Cuts, in the Midst of a Contentious Gubernatorial Race." *Chronicle of Higher Education* 34: 24 + .

———. 25 November 1987g. "Major Changes Seen Needed for Colleges to Attract Minorities." *Chronicle of Higher Education* 34: 1 + .

———. 25 February 1987h. "Most State Officials Shun Uniform Tests as a Way to Measure Progress of Students." *Chronicle of Higher Education* 33: 25 + .

———. 1 April 1987i. "Oklahoma's Governor and College Chancellor Clash over Shutting Institutions, Cutting Budgets, Ethics." *Chronicle of Higher Education* 33: 19 + .

———. 8 April 1987j. "Powerful Lieutenant Governor Helps Texas Colleges Avert Massive Fund Cuts." *Chronicle of Higher Education* 33: 1 + .

———. 6 May 1987k. "Recruiting Plans Found Lacking at Many Colleges in States Where Desegregation Plans Have Expired." *Chronicle of Higher Education* 33: 19 +

———. 18 February 1987l. "States' Midyear Budget Cuts Wreak Havoc on Campuses; Northeast Alone Is Spared." *Chronicle of Higher Education* 33: 19 + .

———. 3 June 1987m. "States Trying to Assess the Effectiveness of Highly Touted Economic Programs." *Chronicle of Higher Education* 33: 19 + .

———. 21 January 1987n. "Three New Chancellors of State Systems Try to Balance Academic Autonomy with Inevitable Political Pressures." *Chronicle of Higher Education* 33: 18–19.

———. 17 June 1987o. "West Virginia's College Presidents Are Selfish and Its Regents Inept, Ex-Chancellor Asserts." *Chronicle of Higher Education* 33: 15 + .

———. 2 March 1988a. "Governors Caution U.S. against preempting Savings' Efforts." *Chronicle of Higher Education* 34: 17 + .

———. 23 March 1988b. "IRS Ruling Advances Michigan Tuition Plan but Could Quash Other States' Programs." *Chronicle of Higher Education* 34: 1 + .

———. 13 April 1988c. "Maryland Chancellor's Departure Laid to Frustration over Plan to Reorganize State's University System." *Chronicle of Higher Education* 34: 23 + .

———. 18 May 1988d. "State College Officials Call Public's Panic over Fears Needless." *Chronicle of Higher Education* 34: 1 + .

Johnson, Eldon L. 1987. "The 'Other Jeffersons' and the State University Idea." *Journal of Higher Education* 58(2): 127–50.

Johnson, Janet R., and Lawrence R. Marcus. 1986. *Blue Ribbon Commissions and Higher Education: Changing Academe from the Outside*. ASHE-ERIC Higher Education Report No. 2. Washington, D.C.: Association for the Study of Higher Education. ED 272 115. 111 pp. MF–$1.07; PC–$12.07.

Johnson, Lynn G. 1984. *The High-Technology Connection: Academic/Industrial Cooperation for Economic Growth*. ASHE-ERIC Higher Education Report No. 6. Washington, D.C.: Association for the Study of Higher Education. ED 255 130. 129 pp. MF–$1.07; PC–$14.01.

Jones, Dennis P. 1984. *Higher Education Budgeting at the State Level: Concepts and Principles*. Boulder, Colo.: National Center for Higher Education Management Systems. ED 256 625. 120 pp. MF–$1.07; PC–$12.07.

Jones, E. Terrence. 1984. "Public Universities and the New State Politics." *Educational Record* 65(3): 10–12.

Kearney, Richard C. 1987. "How a 'Weak' Governor Can Be Strong." *Journal of State Government* 60(4): 150–56.

Kells, H.R. 1986. "The Second Irony: The System of Institutional Evaluation of Higher Education in the United States." *International Journal of Management in Higher Education* 10(2): 140–49.

Kennedy, Richard. 1981. "Taking Your Case to the State." *CASE Currents* 7(1): 12–14.

Kerr, Clark. 1982. "The Uses of the University, Two Decades Later, Postscript 1982." *Change* 14(7): 23–31.

———. 1985. "The States and Higher Education: Changes Ahead." *State Government* 58(2): 45–50.

Ketter, Robert L. 1978. "By Hemp or by Silk, the Outcome Is the Same." In *Government Regulation of Higher Education*, edited by Walter C. Hobbs. Cambridge, Mass.: Ballinger.

Kirkpatrick, Samuel A., and Lawrence K. Pettit. 1984. "Statewide Postsecondary Education Boards: An Empirical Assessment of Composition, Recruitment, Roles, and Responsibilities." Paper presented at the Conference on Postsecondary Education of the American Educational Research Association and the Association for the Study of Higher Education, October, San Francisco, California.

Kohn, Patricia F., and Kenneth P. Mortimer. 1983. "Selecting Effective Trustees." *Change* 15(5): 30–37.

Krotseng, Marsha V. 1987. "The 'Education Governor': Political Packaging or Public Policy?" Paper presented at the annual meeting of the Association for the Study of Higher Education, November, Baltimore, Maryland. ED 292 401. 36 pp. MF–$1.07; PC not available EDRS.

Lanchantin, Meg. 1986. *Trends in Student Aid: 1980 to 1986*. New

York: College Entrance Examination Board. ED 273 179. 16 pp. MF–$1.07; PC–$3.85.

Lapovsky, Lucie, and Sandra Allard. 1986. "State Support to Private Higher Education." In *Values in Conflict: Funding Priorities for Higher Education*, edited by Mary P. McKeown and Kern Alexander. Cambridge, Mass.: Ballinger.

Lawrence, Judith K., and Kenneth C. Green. 1980. *A Question of Quality: The Higher Education Ratings Game*. AAHE-ERIC Higher Education Report No. 5. Washington, D.C.: American Association for Higher Education. ED 192 667. 76 pp. MF–$1.07; PC–$10.13.

Lederman, Douglas. 23 September 1987. "Act to Reform Schools, Chiefs of 37 Colleges Urge All Presidents." *Chronicle of Higher Education* 34: 1+.

Lee, Eugene C., and Frank M. Bowen. 1971. *The Multicampus University*. New York: McGraw-Hill.

———. 1975. *Managing Multicampus Systems*. San Francisco: Jossey-Bass.

Leslie, Larry L. 1984. "Changing Patterns in Student Financing of Higher Education." *Journal of Higher Education* 55(3): 313–46.

Leslie, Larry L., and Paul T. Brinkman. 1987. "Student Price Response in Higher Education." *Journal of Higher Education* 58(2): 181–204.

Leslie, Larry L., and Garey Ramey. 1986. "State Appropriations and Enrollments: Does Enrollment Growth Still Pay?" *Journal of Higher Education* 57(1): 1–19.

Leventhal, Ruth. 31 May 1988. "Higher Education and Economic Development: Influencing Urban and Rural Development in Pennsylvania." *Memo to the President*. Washington, D.C.: American Association of State Colleges and Universities 28(10).

Levy, Daniel. 1982. "Private versus Public Financing of Higher Education: U.S. Policy in Comparative Perspective." *Higher Education* 11(6): 607–28.

Lincoln, Yvonna S. 1988. "Can Somebody Give Me a Hand Here? Program Review, Accreditation Processes, and Outcomes Assessment as the Straws That Are Breaking the Camel's Back." Paper presented at the annual meeting of the Association for the Study of Higher Education, November, St. Louis, Missouri.

Lindsey, Quentin W. 1985. "Industry/University Research Cooperation: The State Government Role." *Journal of the Society of Research Administrators* 17(2): 85–90.

Longanecker, David A. 1988. "Is There a Positive Side to Cost Containment?" *Grapevine* No. 347. Normal: Illinois State Univ., Center for Higher Education.

McCain, Nina. 16 July 1986. "Massachusetts Governor, Regents Clash over Choice of New Chancellor." *Chronicle of Higher Education* 32: 17.

McCoy, Marilyn. 1983. "The Adoption of Budget Flexibility in Colorado: Its Consequences for the University of Colorado." In *Management Flexibility and State Regulation in Higher Education*, edited by James R. Mingle. Atlanta: Southern Regional Education Board. ED 234 705. 65 pp. MF–$1.07; PC–$7.73.

———. 1984. "State Deregulation and Management Flexibility." *AAHE Bulletin* 36(10): 3–8.

McGuinness, Aims C., Jr. 1986. "The Search for More Effective State Policy Leadership in Higher Education." ECS Working Paper PS-86-1. Denver: Education Commission of the States.

———. 1987. "Analysis of Plans for Higher Education in Maryland." Denver: Education Commission of the States.

———. 1988. *State Postsecondary Education Structures Handbook.* No. PS-87-2. Denver: Education Commission of the States.

McGuinness, Aims C., Jr., Frank M. Bowen, Carol M. Boyer, and Dennis Jones. 1988. "Enhancing the System: Options for Improving Organizational Relations among Rhode Island Public Institutions of Higher Education." Report prepared for the Rhode Island Board of Governors. Denver: Education Commission of the States.

McHenry, K.W. 1985. "University-Industry Research Cooperation: An Industrial View." *Journal of the Society of Research Administrators* 17(2): 31–43.

Madrid, Arturo. 1988. "Quality and Diversity." *AAHE Bulletin* 40(10): 8–11. HE 021 925. 17 pp. MF–$1.07; PC–$3.85.

Magrath, C. Peter, Robert L. Egbert, and Associates. 1987. *Strengthening Teacher Education*. San Francisco: Jossey-Bass.

Mangieri, John N., and John W. Arnn. 1986. "Mapping Out Education Reform: State Systems Come under Scrutiny." *Educational Record* 67(4): 36–41.

Marchese, Theodore J. 1987. "Third Down, Ten Years to Go." *AAHE Bulletin* 40(4): 3–8. HE 021 925. 17 pp. MF–$1.07; PC–$3.85.

Marshall, Catherine. 1985. "Policymakers' Assumptive Worlds: Informal Structures in State Education Policymaking." Paper presented at the annual meeting of the American Education Research Association, April, Chicago, Illinois. ED 274 101. 64 pp. MF–$1.07; PC–$7.73.

Martorana, S.V., and James K. Broomall. 1983. "State, Federal Lawmakers Must Hear from Colleges." *Community and Junior College Journal* 53(6): 18–20.

Maryland Legislative Black Caucus. 1987. "Position Paper on Quality and Equity." Annapolis, Md.: Author.

Matsler, Franklin G. 1988. "The Inconsistencies of State Support for Higher Education." *Grapevine* No. 345. Normal: Illinois State Univ., Center for Higher Education.

Matthews, Jana B., and Rolf Norgaard. 1984. *Managing the Partnership between Higher Education and Industry*. Boulder, Colo.: National Center for Higher Education Management Systems. ED 246 823. 253 pp. MF–$1.07; PC–$24.54.

Melchiori, Gerlinda S. 1982. *Planning for Program Discontinuance*. AAHE-ERIC Higher Education Report No. 5. Washington, D.C.: American Association for Higher Education. ED 224 451. 58 pp. MF–$1.07; PC–$7.73.

Miller, Richard I., and Robert J. Barak. 1986. "Rating Undergraduate Program Review at the State Level." *Educational Record* 67(2–3): 42–46.

Millett, John D. 1984. *Conflict in Higher Education: State Government Coordination versus Institutional Independence*. San Francisco: Jossey-Bass.

Mingle, James R. 1987. *Trends in Higher Education Participation and Success*. Denver: Education Commission of the States.

———. 1988. "Effective Coordination of Higher Education: What Is It? Why Is It So Difficult to Achieve?" *Issues in Higher Education* No. 23. Atlanta: Southern Regional Education Board.

Mingle, James R., ed. 1983. *Management Flexibility and State Regulation in Higher Education*. Atlanta: Southern Regional Education Board. ED 234 705. 65 pp. MF–$1.07; PC–$7.73.

Mingle, James R., and Associates. 1981. *Challenges of Retrenchment*. San Francisco: Jossey-Bass.

Mitchell, Brad L. 1987. "Higher Education Reform and Ad Hoc Committees: A Question of Legitimacy." *Review of Higher Education* 11(2): 117–35.

Mooney, Carolyn J. 22 October 1986. "Higher Education Gets a High Priority in Many Gubernatorial Races This Fall." *Chronicle of Higher Education* 33: 15 + .

———. 29 April 1987a. "Feisty New Governor Has Arizona Colleges Worried." *Chronicle of Higher Education* 33: 21–22.

———. 14 October 1987b. "No Joke: Higher Education in New Jersey Thrives along with State's Booming Economy." *Chronicle of Higher Education* 34: 20 + .

———. 25 March 1987c. "One Hectic Day in the Life of a State College Lobbyist in Utah: How Weber State's Bob DeBoer Tries to Stave Off a Budget Cut." *Chronicle of Higher Education* 33: 21 + .

———. 8 July 1987d. "Private Colleges Mount Intensified Campaigns for State Aid." *Chronicle of Higher Education* 33: 1 + .

———. 15 April 1987e. "West Virginia Regents Spar with Governor over Huge Cutback and How to Achieve It." *Chronicle of Higher Education* 33: 23 + .

Morgan, Anthony W., and Brad L. Mitchell. 1985. "The Quest for Excellence: Underlying Policy Issues." *Higher Education: Hand-*

book of Theory and Research, vol. 1, edited by John C. Smart. New York: Agathon Press.

Morgan, Patrick M. 1983. "Higher Education in a Conservative Era." *Educational Record* 64(1): 10–17.

Mortimer, Kenneth P. 1972. *Accountability in Higher Education.* AAHE-ERIC Higher Education Report No. 1. Washington, D.C.: American Association for Higher Education. ED 058 465. 60 pp. MF–$1.07; PC–$7.73.

———. 1986. "The Organization and Administration of American Multicampus Systems: The Case of Pennsylvania State University." Paper presented at an international workshop of the Univ. of the Aegean, June, Athens, Greece.

———. 1987. "State Policy and Institutional Autonomy: Intrusion or Integration?" Keynote speech at a meeting of the Association for the Study of Higher Education, November, Baltimore, Maryland.

Moynihan, Daniel Patrick. 1980. "State vs. Academe." *Harper's* 261(1567): 31–40.

Nason, John W. 1980. "Responsibilities of the Governing Board." In *Handbook of College and University Trusteeship,* edited by Richard T. Ingram and Associates. San Francisco: Jossey-Bass.

———. 1984. "Trustee Responsibilities." Prepared for a meeting of the Association of Governing Boards of Universities and Colleges, January, Washington, D.C.

National Conference of Lieutenant Governors. 1986. *Living on the Leading Edge.* Lexington, Ky.: Council of State Governments.

National Governors' Association. 1986. *Time for Results: The Governors' 1991 Report on Education.* Washington, D.C.: Author.

———. 1987a. *Jobs, Growth, and Competitiveness.* Washington, D.C.: Author.

———. 1987b. *Results in Education: 1987.* Washington, D.C.: Author. UD 026 385. 82 pp. MF–$1.07; PC–$10.13.

Newell, Barbara. 1986. "How Florida Handled Admission Standards." *AGB Reports* 28(1): 21–23.

Newman, Frank. 1985a. *Higher Education and the American Resurgence.* A Carnegie Foundation Special Report. Lawrenceville, N.J.: Princeton Univ. Press.

———. 1985b. "Rising Expectations: Can States Help Renew Quality?" *Change* 17(6): 13–15.

———. 1987a. *Choosing Quality: Reducing Conflict between the State and the University.* Denver: Education Commission of the States.

———. 1987b. "Taking Charge of Ourselves." *Currents* 13(2): 6–12.

Nowlan, James D., Christopher O. Ross, and Mildred A. Schwartz. 1984. "The University of Illinois Trustees: 'Invisible' Statewide

Candidates?'' Urbana: Univ. of Illinois, Institute of Government and Public Affairs.

O'Keefe, Michael. 1985. "Self-Inflicted Laryngitis." *Change* 17(2): 11–13.

———. 1986. "A New Look at College Costs: Where Does the Money Really Go?" *Change* 19(6): 12–34.

Olliver, James. 1982. "The States and Independent Higher Education: Policies, Programs, and Planning for the 1980s." Washington, D.C.: National Institute of Independent Colleges and Universities. ED 219 991. 21 pp. MF–$1.07; PC–$3.85.

O'Neill, Joseph P. 1981. "State Role in Private College Closings." In *Challenges of Retrenchment*, edited by James R. Mingle. San Francisco: Jossey-Bass.

Osborne, David. 1987. *Economic Competitiveness: The States Take the Lead*. Washington, D.C.: Economic Policy Institute.

Peebles, Lynn. 18 December 1985a. "Council Expects State Policy Makers Rather than Educators to Assume the Main Roles in Reform of Higher Education." *Chronicle of Higher Education* 31: 10.

———. 25 October 1985b. "New Strains Found between Public and Private Colleges." *Chronicle of Higher Education* 31: 11 + .

———. 7 May 1986a. "Concern about Quality Prompts States to Undertake Reviews of Their Colleges." *Chronicle of Higher Education* 32: 13 + .

———. 22 January 1986b. "Many Governors Place Aid for Colleges among Their Top Objectives This Year." *Chronicle of Higher Education* 31: 13 + .

Peterson, Paul E. 1983. "Did the Education Commission Say Anything?" *Brookings Review* 2(2): 3–11.

Pettit, Lawrence K. 1987. "Ambiguities in the Administration of Public University Systems." In *When Colleges Lobby States*, edited by Leonard E. Goodall. Washington, D.C.: American Association of State Colleges and Universities. ED 293 384. 264 pp. MF–$1.07; PC not available EDRS.

Pettit, Lawrence K., and Samuel A. Kirkpatrick. 1984a. "Combat Leaders without Troops." *Educational Record* 65(3): 4–7.

———. 1984b. "Postsecondary Educational Governance among the States: An Introduction to the Roles of the Statewide Executive Officers and Their Boards." Paper presented at the annual meeting of the American Educational Research Association, April, New Orleans, Louisiana. ED 243 368. 46 pp. MF–$1.07; PC–$5.79.

Petty, Gary F., and William E. Piland. 1985. "The Illinois Public Community College Board Members." In *Active Trusteeship for a Changing Era*, edited by Gary F. Petty. New Directions for Community Colleges No. 51. San Francisco: Jossey-Bass.

Phillips, John. 1985. "The Missing Factor in the Equation: Public Policy." *National Forum* 65(3): 28–31.

Pickens, William. 1986. "State Budgeting for Higher Education: Is There an Ideal Approach?" *Grapevine* No. 325. Normal: Illinois State Univ., Center for Higher Education.

Pipho, Chris. 1988. "The Changing State Legislature." *Phi Delta Kappan* 69(5): 326–27.

Pound, William T. 1986. "The State Legislatures." *Book of the States* 26: 76–81.

Preer, Jean L. 1981. *Minority Access to Higher Education*. AAHE-ERIC Higher Education Report No. 1. Washington, D.C.: American Association for Higher Education. ED 207 474. 55 pp. MF–$1.07; PC–$7.73.

Quehl, Gary H. 1988. *Higher Education and the Public Interest: A Report to the Campus*. Washington, D.C.: Council for Advancement and Support of Education.

Rabineau, Louis. 1984. "How to Work with Governors, Legislators." *AGB Reports* 26(5): 26–27.

Rauh, Morton A. 1969. *The Trusteeship of Colleges and Universities*. New York: McGraw-Hill.

Recer, J. Dan. 1980. "Don't Doubt Your Clout." *CASE Currents* 6(11): 14–16.

Richardson, Richard C., Jr., and Louis W. Bender. 1987. *Fostering Minority Access and Achievement in Higher Education: The Role of Urban Community Colleges and Universities*. San Francisco: Jossey-Bass.

Richardson, Richard C., Jr., and Elizabeth Fisk Skinner. 1988. "Making It in a Major University: The Minority Graduate's Perspective." *Change* 20(3): 34 +.

Robb, Charles S. 1982. "Higher Education, the New Federalism, and the States." *Change* 14(4): 38–42.

Sedlak, Michael, and Steven Schlossman. 1986. *Who Will Teach? Historical Perspectives on the Changing Appeal of Teaching as a Profession*. Report R-3472-CSTP. Santa Monica, Cal.: Rand Corporation. ED 292 184. 61 pp. MF–$1.07; PC not available EDRS.

Seneca, Joseph J., and Michael K. Taussig. 1987. "Educational Quality, Access, and Tuition Policy at State Universities." *Journal of Higher Education* 58(1): 25–37.

Shaw, Kenneth A., and James M. Brown. 1981. "How to Hire a Government Relations Director." *CASE Currents* 8(8): 34–35.

Skinner, Elizabeth Fisk, and Richard C. Richardson, Jr. 1988. "Resolving Access/Quality Tensions: Minority Participation and Achievement in Higher Education." Paper presented at the annual meeting of the Association for the Study of Higher Education, November, St. Louis, Missouri.

Skinner, Patricia, and Jonathan Tafel. 1986. "Promoting Excellence in

Undergraduate Education in Ohio." *Journal of Higher Education* 57(1): 93–105.

Slaughter, Sheila, and Edward T. Silva. 1985. "Toward a Political Economy of Retrenchment: The American Public Research Universities." *Review of Higher Education* 8(4): 295–318.

Sloan Commission on Government and Higher Education. 1980. *A Program for Renewed Partnership*. Cambridge, Mass.: Ballinger. ED 184 497. 61 pp. MF–$1.07; PC–$7.73.

Spruill, Ann. 1986. "State Policy on Partnerships between Higher Education and Industry." ECS Working Paper PS-86-2. Denver: Education Commission of the States.

State Board for Higher Education, Office of the Commissioner. 1987. "Four Alternatives for Postsecondary Education Reorganization in Maryland: An Analysis." Paper prepared by the Commissioner of Higher Education, Annapolis, Maryland.

State Higher Education Executive Officers. 1987a. *A Difference of Degrees: State Initiatives to Improve Minority Student Achievement*. Denver: Author. ED 287 355. 75 pp. MF–$1.07; PC–$7.73.

———. 1987b. *Focus on Minorities: Synopsis of State Higher Education Initiatives*. Denver: Education Commission of the States. ED 287 403. 39 pp. MF–$1.07; PC–$5.79.

———. 1987c. "A Statement of Policy by the State Higher Education Executive Officers on Program and Institutional Assessment." Denver: Author.

Tancredo, Thomas G. 1984. "State Deregulation and Management Flexibility." *AAHE Bulletin* 36(10): 3–8. ED 254 131. 7 pp. MF–$1.07; PC–$3.85.

Taylor, Barbara E. 1987. *Working Effectively with Trustees*. ASHE-ERIC Higher Education Report No. 2. Washington, D.C.: Association for the Study of Higher Education. ED 284 509. 141 pp. MF–$1.07; PC–$14.01.

Thompson, Fred, and William Zumeta. 1981. "A Regulatory Model of Governmental Coordinating Activities in the Higher Education Sector." *Economics of Education Review* 1(1): 27–52.

Troxler, G. William, and H. Judith Jarrell. 1984. "Capital Ideas." *Currents* 10(3): 46–48.

Tucker, Marc S. 1986. "State Economic Development and Education: A Framework for Policy Development." In *Living on the Leading Edge*. Lexington, Ky.: Council of State Governments.

U.S. Department of Education, Center for Education Statistics. 1987. *Digest of Education Statistics*. Washington, D.C.: U.S. Government Printing Office. ED 282 359. 424 pp. MF–$1.07; PC–$36.86.

Van de Water, Gordon. 1982. "Emerging Issues in Postsecondary Education, 1981." *Higher Education in the States* 8(1): 1–28. ED 215 621. 82 pp. MF–$1.07; PC–$10.13.

Volkwein, J. Fredericks. 1984. "State Financial Control Practices and Public Universities: Results of a National Study." Paper presented at the annual meeting of the Association for the Study of Higher Education, March, Chicago, Illinois. ED 245 608. 36 pp. MF–$1.07; PC–$5.79.

————. 1986a. "Campus Autonomy and Its Relationship to Measures of University Quality." *Journal of Higher Education* 57(5): 510–28.

————. 1986b. "State Financial Control of Public Universities and Its Relationship to Campus Administrative Elaborateness and Cost: Results of a National Study." *Review of Higher Education* 9(3): 267–86.

————. 1987. "State Regulation and Campus Autonomy." *Higher Education: Handbook of Theory and Research,* vol. 3, edited by John C. Smart. New York: Agathon Press.

————. 1989. "Changes in Quality among Public Universities." *Journal of Higher Education.* Forthcoming.

Wallace, James C. 1987. "Incentives for Improvement in Higher Education. New Jersey: A Case Study." *Grapevine* No. 335. Normal: Illinois State Univ., Center for Higher Education.

Wallhaus, Robert A. 1982. "Process Issues in State-Level Program Reviews." In *Designing Academic Program Reviews*, edited by R. Wilson. New Directions for Higher Education No. 37. San Francisco: Jossey-Bass.

Widmayer, Patricia. 1984. "From Lean Times to Enrollment Declines: The Governor's Commission on the Future of Higher Education in Michigan." Paper presented at the annual meeting of the Association for the Study of Higher Education, March, Chicago, Illinois. ED 247 869. 12 pp. MF–$1.07; PC–$3.85.

Wilensky, Rona. 1988. "Trends in the Public and Independent Sectors of Higher Education." Working Paper No. PS-88-1W. Denver: Education Commission of the States.

Wilson, Blenda. 1988. "Leadership for Higher Education in an Increasingly Political Context." Keynote address at the annual meeting of the Association for the Study of Higher Education, November, St. Louis, Missouri.

Wilson, Robin. 11 November 1987. "Lobbyists and College Presidents Debate Need for Political Action Committee." *Chronicle of Higher Education* 34: 23 + .

Winchester, Ian. 1985. "The Concept of University Autonomy: An Anachronism?" In *The Professoriate-Occupation in Crisis*. Toronto: Ontario Institute for Studies in Education.

Winter, William. 1985. "The Changing Role of the Governor in Higher Education." *State Government* 58(2): 56–58.

Wittstruck, John R., and Stephen M. Bragg. 1988. *Focus on Price:*

Trends in Public Higher Education Tuition and State Support.
Denver: State Higher Education Executive Officers.

Yavorsky, Diane K. 1988. "The State Leadership Role: Assuring
Equal Opportunity in Higher Education." *Journal of State Government* 6(2): 66–68.

Zollinger, Richard A. 1985. "Former Governors Look at Higher
Education: Crucial Issues Facing Academe." *State Government*
58(2): 59–64.

Zumeta, William. 1987. "Increasing Higher Education's Contribution
to Economic Development in Urban and Rural Communities:
Lessons from Washington State." Paper presented at the annual
meeting of the Association for the Study of Higher Education,
November, Baltimore, Maryland. ED 292 377. 57 pp. MF–$1.07;
PC–$7.73.

Zumeta, William, and Kenneth C. Green. 1987. "State Policies and
Independent Higher Education: A Conceptual Framework and Some
Empirical Findings, or Can the States Help the Private Sector Survive?" Paper presented at the annual meeting of the Association
for the Study of Higher Education, February, San Diego, California.
ED 281 454. 89 pp. MF–$1.07; PC–$10.13.

Zumeta, William, and Carol Mock. 1985. "State Policy and Private
Higher Education: A Preliminary Research Report." Paper presented at the annual meeting of the Association for the Study of
Higher Education, March, Chicago, Illinois. ED 259 638. 41 pp.
MF–$1.07; PC–$5.79.

Zusman, Ami. 1986. "Legislature and University Conflict: The Case
of California." *Review of Higher Education* 9(4): 397–418.

Zwingle, J.L. 1980. "Evolution of Lay Governing Boards." In
Handbook of College and University Trusteeship, edited by Richard
T. Ingram. San Francisco: Jossey-Bass.

INDEX

A

AAC (see Association of American Colleges)

Access to education, 83, 85

Accountability

    balance with autonomy, 39, 46, 105

    early watchword, 36

    governmental intrusion, 37–38

    multiple facets, 37

    policy question, 10

    state legislative procedures, 37–38

Accreditation, 88

ACE (see American Council on Education)

Ad hoc committees, 8

Advance Technology Development Center, 59

Alabama: gubernatorial involvement, 22

Alexander, Lamar, 30

Alverno College, 93, 95

American Can Company, 81

American College Testing Service, 54

American Council on Education (ACE), 31, 81

American Indians, 82, 83, 84

Ashcroft, John, 31, 92, 97, 99

Ashcroft Task Force, 92–93, 97

Assessment

    case studies, 98–99

    ECS project, 96–97

    institutional examples/plans, 95, 97

    patterns of response, 100

    policy issue, 111–112

    reform issue, 91–94, 101

    state board actions, 97–98

    state initiatives, 97

    state role, 94–95

Association of American Colleges (AAC), 94

Association of Governing Boards of Universities and Colleges, 66

Associations, 31

Astin, Alexander, 93

Athletics, 22

Authority, 26–27

Autonomy

    balance with accountability, 39, 46, 105

    constitutional, 26

    deregulation, 40–45

    financial management, 41, 42

    procedural, 36

    program review, 91

Hoblitzell, Alan, 10
Hoblitzell Commission, 11
Hughes, Harry, 10

I

Idaho: deregulation, 42
Illinois
        college-business conflict, 63
        grass-roots lobbying, 35
        public/private college relations, 66
        state aid in private sector, 70
        state appropriations, 51
        trustee selection, 14, 15
        tuition savings plans, 56
Impropriety, 29
Incentive funding, 54–55
Incremental financing, 53
Independent College 500 Index, 56
Indiana
        state aid in private sector, 70
        state appropriations, 51
Information brokers, 59
Internal Revenue Service, 35

J

Job training, 58, 63

K

Kean, Thomas, 27, 30, 92, 96
Kentucky
        deregulation, 42
        tuition savings plan, 56

L

Labor development: state priority, 4
Leadership (see also Governors)
        minority access/retention, 85–87
        necessity, 108–109
        state, 1–47, 106–108
Legislative audits, 37
Legislatures
        accountability demands, 37–38
        Colorado action, 42
        potential divisiveness, 12
        revitalization, 27

Partnerships
      business, 59–61, 81
      school-college, 80–81
      state-higher education, 103–104, 112–114
Pell grants, 31, 49, 68
Pennsylvania
      business partnerships, 59, 64–65
      college-business conflict, 63
      economic development partnerships, 108
      private sector enrollment, 69
      public/private college relations, 66
      race relations, 84
Performance audits, 37–38
Performance Funding Project, 54, 94
Persistance: minority, 82–83
Philanthropy, 67
Plains state appropriations, 52
Policy
      issue implications, 109–112
      making, 114–116
Political action committees (PACs), 35
Political factors
      gubernatorial power, 22–27, 29–30
      inappropriate, 106
      private colleges, 69
      regulation, 40–45
      state aid influence, 22
      student aid, 50
      trustee appointment, 14–15
      trustees as conduits, 16
      tuition prepayment, 57
      White House ideology, 31
Power
      governors, 22–27
      veto, 26
Presidents
      dismissal, 29
      governor/legislator communication, 18
      short terms, 36
      trustee role, 16
      vs. bookstore managers, 35
Private colleges
      cooperation with public, 10
      cost increases, 49
      empirical analyses, 69–71
      federal aid, 68

Higher Education and State Governments 149

Technology issues, 58–59
Tennessee
    accountability demands, 37
    Higher Education Commission, 54
    Performance Funding Project, 54, 94
Texas
    governor's involvement, 29
    lobbying, 34–35
    state aid in private sector, 70
Time for Results, 30
Trustees
    composition, 15, 17
    demographics, 14
    lay trusteeship concept, 13
    minorities, 17
    roles and responsibilities, 13–14, 16–17, 45
    selection, 14–15
Tuition
    as financial support, 67
    fund, 42
    prepayment, 47, 55–57
    pricing, 47–49
    relationship to student aid, 70

U

Undergraduate education improvement, 95–96
University of California at Los Angeles, 70
University of Connecticut, 42
University of Georgia, 22
University of Illinois, 15
University of Maryland, 3, 11
University of Miami, 34
University of Michigan, 9
University of North Carolina, 22
University of Tennessee–Knoxville, 93, 95
Utah
    lobbying, 34
    private sector enrollment, 69

V

Venture capital, 59
Vermont: private sector enrollment, 69
Veto power, 26
Virginia
    assessment approach, 99
    Fund for Excellence, 54

ASHE-ERIC HIGHER EDUCATION REPORTS

Since 1983, the Association for the Study of Higher Education (ASHE) and the ERIC Clearinghouse on Higher Education, a sponsored project of the School of Education and Human Development at The George Washington University, have cosponsored the ASHE-ERIC Higher Education Report series. The 1988 series is the seventeenth overall, with the American Association for Higher Education having served as cosponsor before 1983.

Each monograph is the definitive analysis of a tough higher education problem, based on thorough research of pertinent literature and institutional experiences. After topics are identified by a national survey, noted practitioners and scholars write the reports, with experts reviewing each manuscript before publication.

Eight monographs (10 monographs before 1985) in the ASHE-ERIC Higher Education Report series are published each year, available individually or by subscription. Subscription to eight issues is $60 regular; $50 for members of AERA, AAHE, and AIR; $40 for members of ASHE (add $10.00 for postage outside the United States).

Prices for single copies, including 4th class postage and handling, are $15.00 regular and $11.25 for members of AERA, AAHE, AIR, and ASHE ($10.00 regular and $7.50 for members for 1985 to 1987 reports, $7.50 regular and $6.00 for members for 1983 and 1984 reports, $6.50 regular and $5.00 for members for reports published before 1983). If faster postage is desired for U.S. and Canadian orders, add $1.00 for each publication ordered; overseas, add $5.00. For VISA and MasterCard payments, include card number, expiration date, and signature. Orders under $25 must be prepaid. Bulk discounts are available on orders of 15 or more reports (not applicable to subscriptions). Order from the Publications Department, ASHE-ERIC Higher Education Reports, The George Washington University, One Dupont Circle, Suite 630, Washington, D.C. 20036-1183, or phone us at 202/296-2597. Write for a publications list of all the Higher Education Reports available.

1988 ASHE-ERIC Higher Education Reports

1. The Invisible Tapestry: Culture in American Colleges and Universities
   George D. Kuh and Elizabeth J. Whitt

2. Critical Thinking: Theory, Research, Practice, and Possibilities
   Joanne Gainen Kurfiss

3. Developing Academic Programs: The Climate for Innovation
   Daniel T. Seymour

4. Peer Teaching: To Teach Is to Learn Twice
   Neal A. Whitman

5. Higher Education and State Governments: Renewed Partnership, Cooperation, or Competition?
   Edward R. Hines

1987 ASHE-ERIC Higher Education Reports

1. Incentive Early Retirement Programs for Faculty: Innovative Responses to a Changing Environment
   Jay L. Chronister and Thomas R. Kepple, Jr.

2. Working Effectively with Trustees: Building Cooperative Campus Leadership
   Barbara E. Taylor

3. Formal Recognition of Employer-Sponsored Instruction: Conflict and Collegiality in Postsecondary Education
   Nancy S. Nash and Elizabeth M. Hawthorne

4. Learning Styles: Implications for Improving Educational Practices
   Charles S. Claxton and Patricia H. Murrell

5. Higher Education Leadership: Enhancing Skills through Professional Development Programs
   Sharon A. McDade

6. Higher Education and the Public Trust: Improving Stature in Colleges and Universities
   Richard L. Alfred and Julie Weissman

7. College Student Outcomes Assessment: A Talent Development Perspective
   Maryann Jacobi, Alexander Astin, and Frank Ayala, Jr.

8. Opportunity from Strength: Strategic Planning Clarified with Case Examples
   Robert G. Cope

1986 ASHE-ERIC Higher Education Reports

1. Post-tenure Faculty Evaluation: Threat or Opportunity?
   Christine M. Licata

2. Blue Ribbon Commissions and Higher Education: Changing Academe from the Outside
   Janet R. Johnson and Lawrence R. Marcus

3. Responsive Professional Education: Balancing Outcomes and Opportunities
   Joan S. Stark, Malcolm A. Lowther, and Bonnie M.K. Hagerty

4. Increasing Students' Learning: A Faculty Guide to Reducing Stress among Students
   Neal A. Whitman, David C. Spendlove, and Claire H. Clark

5. Student Financial Aid and Women: Equity Dilemma?
   Mary Moran

6. The Master's Degree: Tradition, Diversity, Innovation
   Judith S. Glazer

7. The College, the Constitution, and the Consumer Student: Implications for Policy and Practice
   Robert M. Hendrickson and Annette Gibbs

8. Selecting College and University Personnel: The Quest and the Questions
   Richard A. Kaplowitz

1985 ASHE-ERIC Higher Education Reports

1. Flexibility in Academic Staffing: Effective Policies and Practices
   Kenneth P. Mortimer, Marque Bagshaw, and Andrew T. Masland

2. Associations in Action: The Washington, D.C., Higher Education Community
   Harland G. Bloland

3. And on the Seventh Day: Faculty Consulting and Supplemental Income
   Carol M. Boyer and Darrell R. Lewis

4. Faculty Research Performance: Lessons from the Sciences and Social Sciences
   John W. Creswell

5. Academic Program Reviews: Institutional Approaches, Expectations, and Controversies
   Clifton F. Conrad and Richard F. Wilson

6. Students in Urban Settings: Achieving the Baccalaureate Degree
   Richard C. Richardson, Jr., and Louis W. Bender

7. Serving More Than Students: A Critical Need for College Student Personnel Services
   Peter H. Garland

8. Faculty Participation in Decision Making: Necessity or Luxury?
   Carol E. Floyd

1984 ASHE-ERIC Higher Education Reports

1. Adult Learning: State Policies and Institutional Practices
   K. Patricia Cross and Anne-Marie McCartan

2. Student Stress: Effects and Solutions
   Neal A. Whitman, David C. Spendlove, and Claire H. Clark

3. Part-time Faculty: Higher Education at a Crossroads
   Judith M. Gappa

4. Sex Discrimination Law in Higher Education: The Lessons of the Past Decade
   J. Ralph Lindgren, Patti T. Ota, Perry A. Zirkel, and Nan Van Gieson

5. Faculty Freedoms and Institutional Accountability: Interactions and Conflicts
   Steven G. Olswang and Barbara A. Lee

6. The High-Technology Connection: Academic/Industrial Cooperation for Economic Growth
   Lynn G. Johnson

7. Employee Educational Programs: Implications for Industry and Higher Education
   Suzanne W. Morse

8. Academic Libraries: The Changing Knowledge Centers of Colleges and Universities
   Barbara B. Moran

9. Futures Research and the Strategic Planning Process: Implications for Higher Education
   James L. Morrison, William L. Renfro, and Wayne I. Boucher

10. Faculty Workload: Research, Theory, and Interpretation
    Harold E. Yuker

1983 ASHE-ERIC Higher Education Reports

1. The Path to Excellence: Quality Assurance in Higher Education
   Laurence R. Marcus, Anita O. Leone, and Edward D. Goldberg

2. Faculty Recruitment, Retention, and Fair Employment: Obligations and Opportunities
   John S. Waggaman

3. Meeting the Challenges: Developing Faculty Careers*
   Michael C.T. Brookes and Katherine L. German

4. Raising Academic Standards: A Guide to Learning Improvement
   Ruth Talbott Keimig

5. Serving Learners at a Distance: A Guide to Program Practices
   Charles E. Feasley

6. Competence, Admissions, and Articulation: Returning to the Basics in Higher Education
   Jean L. Preer

7. Public Service in Higher Education: Practices and Priorities
   Patricia H. Crosson

8. Academic Employment and Retrenchment: Judicial Review and Administrative Action
   Robert M. Hendrickson and Barbara A. Lee

9. Burnout: The New Academic Disease*
   Winifred Albizu Meléndez and Rafael M. de Guzmán

10. Academic Workplace: New Demands, Heightened Tensions
    Ann E. Austin and Zelda F. Gamson

*Out-of-print. Available through EDRS.

Order Form

QUANTITY   AMOUNT

_____ Please enter my subscription to the 1988 ASHE-
ERIC Higher Education Reports at $60.00, 50%
off the cover price, beginning with Report 1, 1988. _____

_____ Please enter my subscription to the 1989 ASHE-
ERIC Higher Education Reports at $80.00, 33%
off the cover price, beginning with Report 1, 1989. _____

_____ Outside U.S., add $10.00 per series for postage. _____

Individual reports are available at the following prices:
1988 and forward, $15.00 per copy. 1983 and 1984, $7.50 per copy.
1985 to 1987, $10.00 per copy.   1982 and back, $6.50 per copy.

Book rate postage, U.S. only, is included in the price.
For fast U.P.S. shipping within the U.S., add $1.00 per book.
Outside U.S., please add $1.00 per book for surface shipping.
For air mail service outside U.S., add $5.00 per book.
All orders under $25 must be prepaid.

PLEASE SEND ME THE FOLLOWING REPORTS:

QUANTITY   TITLE   AMOUNT
_____ Report NO. ___ (_____)   _____
_____ Report NO. ___ (_____)   _____
_____ Report NO. ___ (_____)   _____
                                        SUBTOTAL: _____
                        POSTAGE (see above) _____
                        TOTAL AMOUNT DUE: _____

Please check one of the following:

☐ Check enclosed, payable to ASHE.
☐ Purchase order attached.
☐ Charge my credit card indicated below:
☐ VISA   ☐ MasterCard

☐☐☐☐☐☐☐☐☐☐☐☐☐☐☐ | | |

Expiration date _____

Name _____

Title _____

Institution _____

Address _____

City _____ State _____ Zip _____

Phone _____ Signature _____

ALL ORDERS SHOULD BE SENT TO:
ASHE-ERIC Higher Education Reports
The George Washington University
One Dupont Circle, Suite 630, Dept. RC
Washington, DC 20036-1183
Phone: 202/296-2597